# The  Pro

**10 Key Concepts To Master The Art Of Sales**

*By Dan E Blaze*

***(A 'Master Sales Manual Series of Books)***

Copyright ® 2014 by
The Suadela Mercury Co.

ISBN-13: 978-1502563040

All rights reserved. No portion of this book may be Reproduced — mechanically, electronically, or by any other means, including photocopying — without written permission of the author or publisher.

All chapter images are the proprietary expression of Shania Janzen-Cox Copyright © 2014

Visit [www.MasterSalesManual.com](www.MasterSalesManual.com) or email [Dan@MasterSalesManual.com](Dan@MasterSalesManual.com) for more information

Copyright © 2014
The Suadela Mercury Co.

## About The Master Sales Manual Series of Books

The Perfect Sales Pro is the first in the Master Sales Manual Series of Books, and is designed only to act as a summary introduction to The Master Sales Manual, and subsequent releases.

All titles in this series are based on proven models and principles as found in psychology, business, marketing and as passed on through professional training courses and seminars. You will not find any advice or suggestion skewed to my own point of view, or the point of view of others… Only cold hard facts, and proven concepts. The series is designed for true professional learning without the use of lengthy stories or multiple examples. If you're ready to dive right in, with information and techniques that you can start using today, then these are the books for you!

The Master Sales Manual Series of Books will take you through a broader view of sales in order to help you develop into a more complete professional. If you've ever been in a real selling situation, then you know that there is more to sales then simply telling others all about the wonderful features and benefits of your product. Sales professionals today need to win the customer over from start to finish.

The Master Sales Manual is the ONLY book that provides an in-depth review of each of the 10 critical skill-sets necessary to become a master at the art of sales. It is essentially a text-book reference guide to sales and adjacent fields of study. It is NOT your regular sales book, and is not designed to entertain you.

*The Master Sales Manual: For the Serious Professional!*

# Contents

Preface .................................................................... 7

Acknowledgements ................................................ 11

Introduction .......................................................... 13

Develop Yourself First ........................................... 17

Understand Your Customers ................................. 23

Market Yourself ..................................................... 75

Prospect For Targets ............................................. 91

Present Like A Master ......................................... 105

Sell Like A Pro ...................................................... 123

Use Persuasive Communication .......................... 143

Build Powerful Relationships .............................. 168

Grow Your Business ............................................. 183

# Preface

I was 23 when I got into sales. My first job selling windows for a national window company. They sat me at a desk with a little black phone, handed me the phone book, and said "ok, call people and sell them windows". Then they explained "first thing is first, set up some appointments to go visit people". "Visit who?" I asked! "Who do I call? Who wants to buy our windows" The answer that echoed to me form across the room was disappointing… "There's the phone book - Start with A". Thank God it was just a local phone book.

It was years later when I got hired with a large call-center that I received my first ounce of REAL training. How to sell… What to Say… How to Say it. They taught me to use features and benefits in succession… Give them a feature, and immediately follow up with a benefit. Just repeat this over and over. At the time, these were advanced sales skills… At least to me.

I remember reading that big companies such as Xerox and IBM would send their Salesforce to be professionally trained. I remember wondering why none of the companies that I worked for (to date) had sent me to any formal sales training. I also remember asking myself over and over again how I could possibly become better at my chosen career.

As I moved from one job to another, I started paying attention to things. I would find the best seller in each job and listen closely to what he's saying, and how he's saying it... To the inflection in his voice... To the words he chose.. And then I would ask a lot of questions. I would often take time out to do this when I should have been working, which caused me many disputes with management. At some point... I decided it just wasn't enough.

THE PROBLEM: Unless you work for some large corporation – Fewer and fewer companies are investing in sales training for their Salesforce... And those who make an attempt to train their sales staff often provide very basic sales skills

So came the time for me to train myself. I started paying for professional training classes with my own funds. I started buying every sales book I could get my hands on. I bought audio tapes and listened to them day in and day out... And after time, some of it started sinking in. My sales skills started developing and I because a much more persuasive individual.

With so much confidence in myself, I took on opportunities as an independent salesperson with a heating and ventilation company. I was introduced to the world of DIY "Do It Yourself"..

THE SECOND PROBLEM!: Sales skills alone, just aren't enough. You need a heck of a lot more than mere sales skills to be a well-rounded professional.

I had to create lead-lists; book appointments; plan and perform sales presentations; persuade them to buy; negotiate the offer; close the deal; and build a referral network. It may not seem like a lot, but I found it to be overwhelming for just one person.

With my new-found sales skills, I sought to teach myself everything I could about being a successful independent salesperson. Very little assistance in the matter was provided by the company (and as I moved to other positions later, I found this to be a growing trend).

I decided to spend years researching methods and techniques of honing every skill necessary to be the Perfect Sales Pro, and I wrote it all in one book entitled "The Master Sales Manual". I wrote the book as a training guide for myself. This book – The Perfect Sales Pro – Is a summary of that research.

# Acknowledgements

**No-one who achieves success does so without acknowledging the help of others.**

- *Alfred North Whitehead*

In acknowledging those who aided in the development and completion of The Perfect Sales Pro, I am really providing a duality of thanks… Additionally thanking those who were there, in heart and body, through the creation of The Master Sales Manual, as it was actually written prior to this book, and it is from those pages that spawned The Perfect Sales Pro.

I would like thank my friends who, through their love and criticism, never gave up – As imaginary as these books were before finally taking shape. A very special thank to Leona (Xin) Liu and Darwin Cox for standing by me through those hard times.

I would also like to thank those whom, through their connections, helped in the marketing promoting of both books.

It is especially important that I thank all prior authors of related books and material, for not having written a book like these before… Thus giving me the insight of what needed to be done for salespeople like myself.

A special thanks to Shania Janzen Cox for the artwork that was provided for the chapter covers, from introductory to chapter 10. As an extremely talented and young digital artist – I hope you continuously let flow the creativity that surges within.

Finally, I want to thank all those who have provided me with the training and knowledge necessary to provide these works… From mentors, to previous authors, to all employers who have allowed me the experience from which I write.

## *Introduction*

$\mathcal{E}$very professional knows that preparation is key to success. Let's face it... People just don't run marathons without warming up first. We don't build houses without a blue-print, and we don't start a business without knowing something about the business we aim to start. Preparation is the preventative measure that averts disaster.

Salespeople are no different. We need to warm up first, build a blue print, and ... Breathe... And then understand a bit about the sales journey we are about to embark on. In this book, you'll find 10 key concepts to building that sales blueprint. The focus this book is not to provide an in-depth analysis of each of those concepts, if that's what you're looking for, then you need The Master Sales Manual. The focus of this, is to touch upon the 10 key concepts in order to broaden your view of sales. Once you recognize these 10 key concepts, you are on your way to becoming the Perfect Sales Pro.

When I was in high-school, working part-time for a small cafe, my school teacher's told me to learn to recognize which skills could be transferred from once job to another. This ideology can be brought to any industry... And if you realize, for example, that sales is not just about selling - Or that being a medical professional requires more than knowledge about medicine - Then you'll realize that being the perfect professional in any field, is quite impossible. Thus we must always learn and seek improvement.

This book is not simply about sales. The 10 key concepts in this book describe the most prominent adjacent fields of study that surround sales. By "adjacent fields" I refer to those subjects that are, in effect, completely separate from sales, and yet necessary for advancement as a great sales professional.

This book was written as a summary of The Master Sales Manual. The Master Sales Manual is an attempt at an in-depth look at these 10 concepts. You can purchase it here:

http://www.mastersalesmanual.com/buynow

SPECIAL NOTE:

Throughout this book, I use a book and pen, like the one to the left. This is my attempt at jumping outside of the script and speaking to you directly. Take special notes here, and enjoy!

# Concept #1
# Develop Yourself First

So… You want to be the Perfect Sales Pro! Well, such a quest doesn't take place in one night… Not even over the weekend. It will take years of effort, energy, learning, and a high degree of attention. Contrary to popular belief, you can't achieve this by improving your sales skills alone. You need to improve every aspect of everything you do. This book will start you on that Journey…

You must first have the right frame of mind… That is… You must fearlessly approach every selling situation with the honest belief that you are going to improve your prospect's quality of life. This unwavering belief must stem from your unlimited confidence in your company, your product and yourself. If you don't believe in your product, or your company, then you honestly shouldn't be selling what you're selling. Confidence comes through knowledge and understanding… So build confidence in your product by understanding it, and more importantly, understanding what it can do for your prospects.

In terms of the development side of preparation, there are three primary considerations to look at: Self-Development is about preparing yourself before encountering sales situations and confronting potential customers. While the majority of this book is about preparation and improving your skillset, this chapter will take a look at the three key areas of self-development: Self-Improvement, Basic Business Skills, and Self-Development itself.

## Self-Improvement

In every situation, you should start by evaluating yourself, before you look at changing others. You can't always change your environment, and you can't always change your prospects, but you can always change yourself – To be better, more adapting, and more efficient.

To be effective in sales and persuasion, you need to have the type of personality that will attract people. Mark McCormack said it best when he proposed: *"All things being equal, people would rather do business with their friends; all things being unequal, people would still rather do business with their friends"*. The Perfect Sales Pro is able to develop strong relationships with prospects and customers who <u>know</u> him, <u>like</u> him and <u>trust</u> him. These are the three pillars to sales success and relationship development.

So ask yourself: What kind of people do others like? Many studies have been performed to answer this question. Here are the basics... People like others who are positive, confident, have a good self-concept and self-esteem, and who are patient and understanding with them. In short, people like others who are generally pleasant to be around, and make them feel good, both in terms of the relationship and in terms of themselves. People also like others who are similar to themselves, and believe that when others are similar to them, they have a better understanding of them. This may sound like a lot, but if you can establish these, you have a great basis for likability, trust, and sales success.

Of course, being in sales, the Perfect Sales Pro must have drive... You have to have drive!!! The insatiable momentum to keep moving forward to reach your goals no matter what happens. Drive consists of three main factors: Persistence, (self) motivation and high enthusiasm. With these, you push forward through any circumstance. Enthusiasm is important in your selling process... Zig

Ziglar, one of America's greatest sales coaches, said "selling is a transfer of enthusiasm".

Most people have trouble developing themselves first, because they don't know which characteristics they need to improve on, and/or they do not have a set definition for those characteristics. I would suggest writing down the characteristics and skills that you wish to develop, and define those characteristics on paper... Use this as a stepping stone to becoming the Perfect Sales Pro.

## Basic Business Skills

If you work for a company or organization, chances are they have set procedures and systems in place to aid you in your success. If they don't, I recommend you systematize as much of your daily, weekly and monthly operations as possible. Begin by having a sales plan, where you can pre-plan what each hour, day and week should hold (Mind you... We both know that nothing ever turns out as planned... Murphy's Law will take effect, but at least you have a general guideline). Once you've created a sales plan, you will have a general idea as to how to begin organizing daily activities. Here are a few keys to help you get started:

### Keep Everything Organized

Organization takes practice and dedication to the cause, but the end result is well worth it. Keep separate files in separate folders - organized in some structural manner to make it easy to find the files you want. Buy a date book or use an online calendar to organize your appointments - and check it often during the day! If you're working with paper, try never to leave loose paper lying around - Always put paper documents back into a file folder, binder or other designated spot. If you have many documents, consider organizing by order of importance, location, or alphabetically. Remind yourself often of the importance of keeping everything in its place as soon as you're finished with it.

**Prioritize Your Activities**

Next, begin to prioritize all of your activities. A simple method of organizing your day is to use the MoSCoW formula: Every night, arrange all the things that you need to do for the next day by classifying them into four categories - Things you Must Do (absolutely); things you Should Do (but are not an absolute necessity for that day); things you Could Do (if you had free time); and things you Would Do (a simple wish list of things you would like to complete). To get one step ahead, you may even consider finishing each day off by ensuring that everything which needs to be organized is ready at the end of today, so that tomorrow morning you can get right at it - Often, beginning the morning by organizing yourself and shuffling papers around, can become a major contributor to procrastination.

**Create Systems**

Lastly, you should look at systematizing all of your activities as best you can. I use to get to the office in the morning, with all of my things organized by level of importance, and then I would look at all things that absolutely must get done and decide where to start. Once I had decided which task I wanted to start with, I began working on that task, and followed-up with all subsequently related tasks... For example, I would begin by calling my first prospect, then writing notes for that call. I would call 40 to 50 prospects and then organize those prospects into pre-set categories according to the events of the call, then scheduling a call back if necessary (Which I wrote in a calendar right away). You can see how one simple task, such as cold-calling, can have many sub-routines! You should have a system to carefully define the order in which each of these sub-routines is performed - and follow that set order for each and every call. In this way, the order that you use today, is the same order that you use tomorrow. Everything you do (as much as possible) should be systematized - This allows the brain to create a neural map of what happens first and what happens next, and quickly recognize any task and its sub-routines, which allows you to become more and more efficient at performing that task.

Being in sales, whether you work for another company or not, you can just as well consider yourself as being in business for yourself. This is especially true if you receive commissions. It is thus your responsibility to ensure that you are as effective and efficient as possible to ensure greater productivity. Define your business... Define how things will be done, in which order they will be performed, which tasks take priority, and how things will be systematized.

# Concept #2
# Understand Your Customers

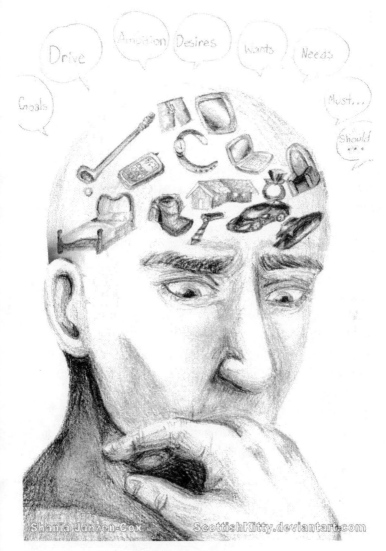

Consumer psychology is all about understanding your customers. What motivates them? What makes them buy? And what makes them choose one product over another? It is by understanding your customers that you will learn how to sell to them. Sure... you could just hand them a product and tell them the price and say "Do you want it or don't you?:" That's how it was done in the good ol' days! Unfortunately, times have changed.

Every so often, salespeople change the way they're selling in order to adapt to the growing demands of consumers, and society in general. They change the way they're selling because the old ways stop working so well - It's not a choice, it's a necessity. Today's consumers are smarter and more proactive than they were yesterday, just as those consumers were smarter than the one's before. Today's consumers have been bombarded by so much advertising, cold-called by so many telemarketers, and approached by so many salespeople, that they have learned a thing or three about how to deal with guys like us! Salespeople - that is.

So how do we adapt? How do we learn new and better ways to sell? How do we evolve into the Perfect Sales Professionals? The answer is simple... Sales professionals know that they must continuously aim to understand their customers (and potential customers). The more we understand them, the greater our ability to adapt our message and presentation to earn their approval (which in turn leads to more sales).

That is what consumer psychology is all about. It includes such factors as

1. What motivates consumers?

2. What influences their decisions?

3. What preferences do consumers have, and how does that effect their decision-making?

4. What process do consumers undertake in their purchase decision?

5. Why would consumers be reluctant to make a purchase?

6. What automatic processes can skew their decision-making?

7. How do they see the world around them, and how does that affect their decision to buy?

The pages in this chapter will give a brief understanding... ..

## Personality Types

Personality profiling involves categorizing people into sub-groups according to the personality traits that they appear to possess. We do this because, while it is true that each person is individual and unique in their overall characteristics, it is impossible for us to fully understand each individual  person we meet, and so an attempt to categorize them provides us with a good basis of understanding individuals, through our understanding of groups (of people). Personality profiling is not new. Probably the earliest model of personality profiling was that of Hippocrates in 460 B.C. Hippocrates, a physician of ancient Greece, described the four temperaments of people as "humors" (moods), which was based on the four elements (earth, fire, air and water). Hippocrates further suggested that one's personality is based on these four humors.

Another interesting case of personality profiling was as used by Dr. Thomas Bond in 1863, the physician who performed the autopsy on Mary Kelly - The last victim of Jack The Ripper... Dr. Bond was able to describe the type of person that the police should be looking for... Of course I understand that he was completely wrong in his profile of Jack the Ripper, but the concept was there. Since then personality profiling has been used by police authorities in catching criminals around the world.

One of the most recognized models of personality profiling today is the "Four-type interpersonal styles" developed by David W. Merill and Roger H. Reid *(Other styles are covered in my next book: The Master Sales Manual)*. Four distinct personality types are recognized. They are: **1. The Driver:** These consumer are business-owners, entrepreneurs and leaders. This type of personality is direct and forceful. (p.s. the Tasmanian Devil is a driver). **2. The Analytical:** These consumers are accountants and strategists. They like to analyze, and take caution to ensure things are correct before proceeding. (p.s. Elmer Fudd goes here).
**3. Expressive:** These consumers are musicians, artists, and salespeople. They like to socialize, and enjoy fast-paced environments. (p.s. the Road Runner is one of these).
**4. Amiable:** These consumers are teachers and social-workers. Their personalities are slow and relationship-driven. (p.s. Santa Clause fits here).

So how does this make a difference you ask? Imagine yourself in conversation with an elderly lady, and you approach her with and expressive style personality... You may give her a heart attack! At best, you'll just scare her off. You might appear eccentric. This is really not the type of personality that elderly ladies want approaching them. You'll need to slow down to her pace, talk at her level of volume and preferably a little softer. Spend a little bit of time building a deeper rapport with her so that she recognizes you in a friendly manner.

Now imagine yourself speaking to a business owner, and you spend an hour building rapport and relationship with him, to show him what could have been said in two minutes. Chances are, he's going to be REALLY upset that you wasted his time... Business people are very busy you know... Usually with business (though not always).

This is not to say that all elderly people or all businessmen are the same, but it should be sufficient to give you a basic idea.

You have to approach people in a manner that suits their personality. Don't expect that they will try to match yours. The better you can match their way of being, the better your chances of creating a good relationship, and selling what you aim to sell... Their way!

## Motivation

Human motivation and consumer buying is very complex. For each decision that we make, there are countless processes going on within our brains. We will take a look at some of these in the next several pages, starting with basic motivation.

Psychologists and sociologists have been studying motivation for years... And just when they were about finished, the corporate world studied motivation just a bit more. Now, they're at it again!

Probably the most pronoun model of human motivation is Abraham Harold Maslow's Hierarchy of Needs. Maslow was an American Psychologist who lived in the 1900's (1908 to 1970), and performed many tests surrounding motivation. He developed the following five-level hierarchy and suggested that each level in the hierarchy (starting with the lowest) must be satisfied before we can move onto the next level.

The five levels are: **1. Physiological Needs** *(Basic Needs)*: Maslow suggests that our primary concern, as humans, is our physiological wellbeing. People want to ensure that they are healthy and in good shape before they consider spending their time or money on anything else. **2. Safety and Security** *(Security Needs)*: Once we have confirmed that we are in good health, our next consideration is whether we have safety and security. **3. Love and Belonging** *(Social Needs)*:

People have an inherent need to belong to something. We naturally need to surround ourselves with others, to groups and to family. This becomes part of our identity and helps us understand ourselves. **4. Self-Esteem** *(Feel-Good Needs)*: Self-esteem is about being happy with who we are. As humans, we are naturally driven to actions that help us do this. Self-esteem becomes a part of the process of self-actualization. **5. Self-Actualization** *(Being Better Needs)*:

Self-actualization is about understand yourself, and becoming all that you can be.

So what does this mean about the way you sell? Stop... for a moment... and consider the following scenario: You're driving down the road and your car breaks down, but that's nothing new as this car has broken down before. Finally, you've decided that it's time to buy a new vehicle. What really runs through your mind at this point?

Most people would begin by dreaming about the kind of car(s) they would like to buy... And then they begin to run through a series of thoughts that may go something like this: The first step would be to check and double check how much money you have sitting in the bank. Then consider all of your necessary expenses and maybe ensure that you have a sufficient amount of funds aside for emergencies. This first step in the thought process satisfies physiological needs.

Once you know how much spare money you have for the purchase of your new automobile, you may consider what type of car to buy (based on what you can afford); What make and model do you want; What store do you buy from; etc. People often make these kind of decisions largely based on trust. Trust... Is a safety need. When we trust something / someone, we feel safer. NOW... let's say you drive up to the car lot, and the salesperson comes out and starts talking to you... and somehow, you have the feeling that he is not being completely truthful to you... What are your chances of buying from him? If you don't trust the salesperson, you may feel he has a hidden agenda, and you may consider buying somewhere else. Trust is not the only factor, however, you may want to research different types of cars, ask your friends for their input and acquire specific information about the cars you are taking into consideration (if it's a used car , check the mileage, previous owners, etc.). Each of these decisions provide you with some degree of safety and security. It is through these processes that you direct yourself to making a decision that is right for you… A decision that you feel comfortable with. Comfort – Is synonymous with "safe".

Once all of your safety concerns are taken care of, you will probably begin to think about how your friends will perceive you in your new car; your family's thoughts; what kind of car your wife would rather buy; etc. If your wife will be driving the car often, you may even buy the type of car she wants to drive. If you belong to a tight social niche, who all drive similar cars, you may buy one of those similar cars. These are the considerations of social needs, or love and belonging needs in Maslow's Hierarchy.

Next, we move up to self-esteem needs. If you're going to spend your money on a brand-new auto, you might as well feel good driving it. If all the previous needs have been satisfied, you'll want to look for the kind of car that makes you feel special. Even if your wife drags you to a Volvo dealership, you'll certainly want to consider the Volvo with the right colors, the right size engine, and definitely the right stereo system (oh, wait a minute, that's just me!). This may be different from one person to the next. While some people may prefer that more powerful engine, others may forgo engine power in return for a powerful stereo, while others still feel wonderful about themselves for buying the world's most frugal vehicle (half the cost per mile would make my wife ecstatic).

Closely tied to self-esteem are self-actualization needs. What does this purchase say about the kind of individual you are? What moral, ethical and righteous needs are being satisfied? These are the type of thoughts that have spawned the growth of electric and hybrid (gas /electric) vehicles. These are the reasons why men give into their wives.

The above examples may be over-simplified... But by understanding what stage your customers are at, you can better understand how to approach them, and how to tailor your message to the way they are thinking. Keep in mind, thought is not static. This means that people are always changing the way they think based on circumstances.

Businesses are no different. When a new business is established, its first concern is survival *(basic needs)*. Then establishing a safety zone within the marketplace *(safety needs)*. Only once this has been established can a company think about belonging to groups and establishing relationships with similar companies *(social needs)*. Then comes concern for reducing costs and risk, and increasing productivity *(feel-good needs)* and finally social awareness *(being better needs)*. While the particular title of each category may require some alteration (for instance – We may call social needs: "Business Relationship Management, "Partnerships" or "Associates and Affiliates") the concept of the category is essentially the same (Business relationship management is still essentially about satisfying social and relationship needs).

Understanding what is important to your customers can help you sell to them. You change the way you present your product(s) according to their basic drives (motivation). You position yourself to be exactly what they want, by first understanding what they want. The methods you use to approach Joe Blow's coffee shop, will not be the same methods you use to approach major franchises such as Tim Horton's or Starbucks, or perhaps Bill Gates - They simply WANT different things... They are NOT motivated by the same things at all.

Once you've defined your target market, define what will motivate them, and why. Recognize that certain types of individuals, certain personalities, certain companies, certain groups, and so on - often have the same motivators. Learn to use your prospect's motivators to your advantage.

## Influences

Motivation alone is often not sufficient to cause people to act. There are always a series of internal and external influences that are involved in the decision making process. McDonald's restaurants understood this, and since their inception, until recently that is, they marketed all their advertising to children, even though children were not the target market. But think about that for a moment... Your child sees an ad on T.V., and suddenly wants to go eat at McDonald's... You say "no" and your child begins to repeat himself, pestering you and nagging to go to McDonald's... You say "no" again and your child throws a temper tantrum, begins to cry and maybe scream a little. Finally you give in and go to McDonald's - Your child has influenced you into going to McDonald's to eat... Children were never the target market... They didn't qualify as a target market because they lacked authority and necessary finances to make the purchase. Children are, however, very very strong influencers. The external influence and emotional pressure of children caused millions of families to visit McDonald's.

Now, McDonald's, along with most fast food restaurants, has changed, and reformed itself to the health conscious individuals that swarm our societies - New Wraps and Salads have been introduced to the menu in attempt to show that fast food restaurants are not just a place to get fat. Why? Because the influence of a changing society who looks for a healthier fast food menu have changed the way the fast food industry operates. The motivation is that of adhering to the laws of supply and demand... They know that the easiest way to sell anybody anything, is to simply give them what they want.

There are two major forms of influences to consider. Internal influence factors and external influence factors. Our examples above included two forms of external influence.

External influence factors can include the influence of family and friends, social status and word of mouth. It may also include legal issues, politics, culture, location, situational changes, or any other form of pressure or influence from the outside world. Time is also considered an external influence factor. There may also be situational influences - For example, a man is more likely to buy a gift for his wife if his she is not with him at the time (It's a gift... She's not supposed to know about it!). The degree to which a buyer likes the seller is also a situational influence. All of these factors may make or break a deal, under particular circumstances. Myself, I truly believe that everything in the universe is dependent upon circumstance.

So be cautious about changes that happen in your prospect's business environment (economic depression, local news, etc.) and re-consider how those changes may affect your prospect's decision to buy.

Internal factors can only be of two types... Psychological, meaning they are related to the way we think; or emotional, related to the way we feel. They may be affected by current events, or by past events. They may also be related to our anticipation of future events. For example, a man may decide not to buy a particular make or model of car based on his experiences with that model in the past - if it consistently broke-down, he will obviously choose a different make or model in the future *(emotional and logical past events)*. If he has children he may consider a minivan *(logical current events)*. If he wants his wife to be happy *(emotional future event)* he will buy whichever model his wife wants to drive.

While we've mentioned a few, there are far too many possible influences to discuss here. However, you can review internal and external factors that affect your own sales. Take some time after each sales attempt and write them down. The more often you do this, the more influence factors you will find. Consider how you planned for and reacted to those influence factors, and then consider how you could plan for and react more effectively.

## Preferences

A person's personal preferences can make all the difference as to whether or not they buy from you. These preferences are directly tied to their personality, and personality differences exist because of a myriad of factors, including: Past experiences, learned (second and third party) experiences, stories passed among peers, culture and location, external influences, and... Well... We just can't count them all here. Let's say it's enough to know that personality is made up of many things, and personality directly influences the way people act or react under different situations and circumstances, thus, because of a person's personality people have certain preferences of how they would like their world to be. These are called "personality preference factors".

Let's relate this to the four-type interpersonal styles described earlier, and how those personalities may react under different types of situations. An Energetic type person may be comfortable in crowds (they like excitement) while an Amiable type person may only feel comfortable in small get-togethers (they like a more personable environment), and Analytic type people may not feel comfortable in crowds at all. Driver and Energetic type personalities may feel comfortable taking risks (for different reasons of course), while Analytic and Amiable type people would not. Driver types would often be alright to receive the benefits of their labor in a future time with greater return, the other three personality types would usually require an immediate return on their labor. This is, however, broad generalization based on the characteristics of those personality types, and these generalizations may not apply to everybody… Many people do not fall directly into one of those generalized categories.

To illustrate this a little better: I've personally changed personality types drastically from the time that I was a young boy. When I was young I was the Amiable type. I had few friends but my friends were very close (and they still are). I was also very shy, disliked crowds, disliked emotional pressure, and disliked challenges. At some point, all that changed – Whether due to necessity, experience, or (in more likely in my case) a simple trigger within the deeper realms of my brain… And my personality went from Amiable to a combination Energetic/Driver type. Now, I make friends wherever I go, and I love being the center of attention (I even have all-white outfits to make sure that happens). I see pressure as a challenge, and I love proving to myself that I can overcome any challenge… Refusing to let any situation get the better of me.

Maybe you've experienced the same type of change in your life. Or maybe you can see the difference between the personality types of two people close to you, and can recognize the difference in how they handle varying situations. These are personality preferences taking effect.

You can find out a lot about a person's personality preferences through effective questioning. Questions that begin with "Which would you prefer…?"; "What's important to you in a…?"; or "Why would you choose…?" can often be very effective.

The Perfect Sales Pro will consider all the situational factors involved with the product or sales process. Take note of the prospect's preference factors that relate to your product or sales process, and approach your prospects and customers in a way that is congruent with their preferences. Use this a means of developing leading-questions. Reposition your offer, and alter your phrasing to match those preferences. Don't just sell people what they want… Sell to them the way they want to be sold to. Speak to them in terms of what they want to hear; and present to them in a way that engages them and captivates their interest.

Are they introvert or extravert? Do they prefer instant gratification, or do they prefer to wait for a bigger return? Do they like challenges and risks, or do they prefer to shy away from challenges and risks? Are they optimists or pessimists? Do they prefer to figure things out for themselves or do they like to have help? Are they motivated more by logic or by emotion? Consider how you can rephrase your statements or questions, as well as how you should change your presentation, based on what you have learned about your prospects! I don't mean to overload you… Take it one step at a time… Change one practice today and one practice tomorrow. I guarantee it will put you on the road to becoming the Perfect Sales Pro.

## The Buying Process

With every buying decision, a complex process occurs in the mind of the buyer causing him to make the purchase, or not make the purchase. A person's buying process may occur either because they recognize a need or problem that must be solved (action-based), or because of an impulse decision (or reaction-based). In this section, we will briefly review both of these.

What's interesting here, as you'll find after careful review, is that even though we like to consider ourselves as intelligent beings, buyers do not make their initial buying decision based on logic. Rather, buying decisions are made based on some form of emotion, and once accepted, that buying decision is then justified using logic, allowing the buyer to feel good about having made the decision.

This is the difference between "needs and "wants". "Needs" are logical and "wants" are emotional. People "need" very few things in this world – Only food, shelter and water. Everything else is a "want"… Everything else is based on some level of desire. Beyond food, shelter and water – All other buying decisions are emotional.

**Standard Buying Process**

What we refer to as the standard buying process is commonly known as the Customer Buying Cycle in sales. The sales industry has attempted to break up a person's buying process into 5 basic steps: 1. Awareness of a need. 2. Researching Potential Solution. 3. Evaluation of Alternatives. 4. Purchase Decision. 5. Purchase. I have added two additional steps not previously mentioned:

Every purchase decision is either preventative or reactive. We are either attempting to prevent something from happening, or we are reacting to something that has already happened. The Standard Buying Process can be either of the two… Most often however, it is still a reactive process. We recognize a problem and feel the need to fix it… Consider, for instance, what would go through your mind if your plumbing no longer worked in your home… What if you were no longer able to turn on the tap? What if the shower wasn't working? Or if the toilet no longer received water to flush properly. Would this be a problem?

Immediately you can recognize the need to have your plumbing fixed. So you begin by isolating the problem... If you are somewhat knowledgeable about home improvements, you may even isolate the specific issue; and if you are not, then you'll be content with the generalization of "it simply doesn't work" and you move on to step 2...

In this step, you'll research alternative solutions. Most people, when they begin this phase of the process, have some type of idea in mind regarding the amount of money they are willing to spend, the amount of time they are willing to allow, and so on. You may begin by researching various local plumbers and asking how much they charge per hour, describing the issue as best as possible and asking how much time they think it will take to fix the issue (Plumbers all charge an 'arm and a leg' an hour). You may contact family and friends and see if any of them know how to repair plumbing. Or you may just ask those family and friends to refer you to a good and reputable plumber. Regardless of any information you receive, you will, however, make your own decision.

The search for the perfect remedy can be extensive or it can be short (or limited), depending on your evaluation of the need or problem and the situation as a whole. The more intense (bigger, costly or important) the need or problem, the more time and effort we tend to involve in the search process. This is possibly because we are afraid of making a bad decision or because we are afraid of the resulting repercussions that a wrong decision may bring.

For example, you would certainly put more time into fixing your home then you would allow for the purchase of stationary supplies for your home office. This is very important, because time plays havoc on our ability to make an intelligent decision. The less time we have to make a decision, the more emotional we become about the decision making process. The opposite also holds true… The more time we take to make the decision, the better our ability to consider all of the factors involved and make an intelligent and logical decision.

If you want to be successful in sales, then you want to limit the amount of time given to your prospects to make a decision. Cause them to make their decision emotionally, and lead them through the emotions you want them to have and toward the purchase of your product.

Once the desire to own the product comes about, and assuming that the buyer can afford the item - before the decision to buy will be an assessment regarding various consequences that immediately come to mind. "What will my wife (or parents or friends) say?" "Will I have enough money for other necessities if I buy this?", "Am I sure this will do the job?" Different consequences are more important to different people (often correlating to their personalities).

If the value of the item outweighs the consequences, the buyer will make the decision to buy. He will then justify in his own mind why he "needs" the item or otherwise why he "should" buy it

Ensure that you've provided the prospect with sufficient value. Remember that value can be associated with anything of importance to the prospect, and does not necessarily need to be financial.

Finally… A decision is made, to either make the purchase or not make the purchase. If the purchase is made, we then feel satisfied the need or problem has been remedied. If we choose not to make the buying decision, we revert to the search process described in the previous paragraph. We may also decide not to make a decision at all, or to postpone the decision based on other factors.

An interesting thing often happens after a purchase decision is made. We then attempt to re-evaluate whether the purchase decision made was the right decision. We may even feel some remorse for having made the decision. This is especially true if we feel the search process was insufficient, or if our purchase decision was too hasty. This is referred to as "buyer's remorse", or "post-purchase syndrome".

This entire process may happen in a split second. Conversely, it may take days, weeks, months or years.

Immediately after a purchase, people are usual excited about having made the purchase, and we tend to give the product excessive attention. Over time, however (and if the product is non-consumable), the excitement begins to fade, and an attentive decline occurs where the interest in the product dissipates.

## The Reactive Buying Process

The Reactive Buying Process is more about impulse buying. This occurs when we make an instantaneous reaction to something resulting in a buying decision.

First, an instant reaction in created. Some new information is presented to the buyer causing an instantaneous influx in emotion. The high-degree of emotion is often caused by the false stimulation of sensory activity – meaning the buyer can actually preconceive experiencing ownership of the product. Have you ever walked by the candy aisle at the grocery store, saw your favorite chocolate bar, and felt as if you could <u>almost</u> taste the chocolate in your mouth? Or maybe that preconception is so strong that your mouth actually begins to water (generate excessive saliva). Quite often, however, the actual resulting experience is not as satisfying as the preconception. This preconception occurs only when we have previously experienced something and when it has had a strong impact on our senses and emotions.

When I was young… Very young… My mother use to tell that my "eyes are bigger than my mouth". This is because, as we sat down to eat dinner, I would load my dinner plate with a lot of my favorite food (usually mash potatoes with butter…mmmm). I would often put so much mash potatoes on my plate that it was a struggle to eat it all. The same thing happens now that I'm older, whether it's at the dinner table or at the mall. The question is… Why?

The emotions that we feel at the time of impulse can cause an imbalance in our brain's activity. We then strive to repair the unbalance, or otherwise "return to normal", and will do "almost" anything for that to happen. This is all causes by a chemical overload related to memory retrieval and feel-good chemicals such as dopamine. The parts of brain that assists in regulating emotion, which include the limbic system (which remembers previous experiences and sets your emotional state) and the prefrontal cortex (responsible for focus, impulse control emotional control, judgment and insight) are prevented from operating normally.

This means, unlike the standard buying process, reactive buying is initiated purely by emotion! In the reactive buying process, there is also no evaluation of alternatives… We go directly to the buying decision. In many cases, buyers don't even consider the consequences of making the purchase, meaning there is no logical component at all. In other cases (such as those individuals who are highly logical in nature), the decision to buy is made, but followed by a quick evaluation of consequences, and then emotion again takes its place. When I realize that I am about to buy on impulse, I hold the product in my hand and walk around with it for about a half an hour, allowing my emotions to subside and logic to sink in. Even if I put it back and decide not to buy, I feel great for having had possession of it for an hour.

You can aid people in making impulse decisions by elevating their emotional state, whether good or bad. Many studies have even showed that people who are depressed are likely to make impulse purchases. The same is true for people who are extremely excited (which explains why we spend so much money when on vacation). You can also aid the process by preventing the emotions from subsiding, which can be one by re-introducing an idea/product often (directly or indirectly).

## Buying Factors

Buying factors are those that directly influence whether or not a person will buy, or will consider buying, a product. By understanding the prospect's buying factors you can establish the criteria that will thus lead to a purchasing decision. Buying factors can usually be broken into two distinct categories: Preliminary and primary buying factors.

Preliminary buying factors are those that influence whether a person will pay attention to a product. Some of the most prominent preliminary factors are: Benefits, personal or business goals (and fulfillment); desire and (more importantly) recurring desire; agitation; trigger events; and suggestion of peers.

Let's look at one of these for example: My favorite - Agitation. People usually seek change after they have become sufficiently agitated by the way things are. There are many forms of agitation, such as irritation, annoyance, anger, frustration, pain, and so on. Let's look at one of these for example... Anger: It was Aristotle, somewhere around 300BC, who first suggested that people will become passionate about one thing, when they have become sufficiently angry about something else (he was referring to its polar opposite). That's what happened to me when I changed my phone service to a new cellular company. The price was amazing for the package deal they provided. However, I was soon experiencing dropped calls, loss of reception in certain areas, and an unbending customer service department. My frustration with their service quickly led to anger, which quickly led to me seeking other alternatives for service. I was even willing to forgo the money that had already spent in favor of better all-around service. I was so angry at the company for the bad service that they had provided... I felt deceived and ignored... And I'm sure I wasn't the only one. Anger was the preliminary factor that caused me to initiate the classic buying cycle... The need: Better service!

Once a person's attention has been directed toward a particular product (even if just for a second), primary buying factors are those that suede the buyer into buying one product over another. Some powerful primary factors include: Value (or perceived value); familiarity with the product, product line or company; exclusivity as related to the product or company (or organization); the immediacy of the need; and how relevant the product is to the buyer's needs and goals. Let's take a look at these a little closer:

**Value**

People are ALWAYS evaluating cost vs. value. We are constantly seeking to spend less and gain more. But cost and value don't necessarily stop at the dollar (although that is a strong component). Cost also consists of anything extra that becomes an element of completing the purchase or making a decision. Cost may include such things as time, effort, the amount of energy spent in making the decision, any frustrations that take place during the decision making or buying process, and so on.

Value is defined as the worth, importance, or usefulness of something. You can quickly see how something may be of value to one person, but not to another – As one person may consider a product to be important, another person may not... The same thing goes for usefulness and worth. Have you ever heard the term "One man's garbage is another man's gold"? This is a perfect example of the difference in "value" in terms of worth. The key to establishing value, therefore, is to determine what is important to each prospect. Earlier we suggested that the easiest way to sell anything to anyone, is to give them what they want... There's a second part to this – How do you know what they want? The answer: Just ask!

## Familiarity

There have been over 200 studies and research concluding that the more familiar we are with something, the more we tend to like it, and the more we feel "attached to it" (emotionally). This is the same with people, places, things, events, and so on. This is partly because a familiarity with something promotes safety and security, and understanding. Another reason is because people seek a sense of consistency in their lives, whether consciously or not – Our brains release extra chemicals when we experience something that is perceived as being new or unfamiliar. The interesting thing about familiarity, is that its effects diminish with time, meaning as time passes between recurrence of events, we become less and less familiar with the people, places and things surrounding that event, and thus the less we tend to like it and the less we feel "attached" to it.

## Exclusivity

The more people feel they are getting something that no-one else is getting, the more they feel "special" – a higher emotional state that most people will do anything to protect. This sense of exclusivity makes people feel they are better than those who do not have the same exclusivity, and appeals directly to the human ego (the part of the unconscious that makes people feel good about themselves). Remember, that people are always striving toward pleasure and away from pain.

Find ways to make people feel special. Use words and phrases that promote this as they will trigger responsiveness to the idea, even if you are not really doing anything special for the customer. Words such as "Just for you"; "Would you like to know a secret?", or "As a special favor".

## Immediacy

Immediacy becomes more important when the prospect has a limited time in which to acquire a product or type of product, or at least one that will fulfill the goals or needs that he has set for himself. In general, the more that time becomes a restraint, the more a prospect will be willing to accept a product or make a purchase, even if that purchase does not fulfill all of the buying factors or buying criteria (covered below).

You want to consider asking the prospect "How soon are you looking to buy your new…?" And "Why is it important to own one by that date?" Try understanding whether the prospect "wants" the product within a specific time frame, or if he feels he "needs" the product within that time frame, as prospects who feel a perceived "need" will buy more readily".

## Relevancy

The more relevant the offer is to the needs, goals and desires of the prospect, the more likely they are to make a buying decision. The thing to remember about relevancy, is that each piece of information you provide that is not relevant to the prospect, will slowly drive him away or cause him to lose interest in your offer. This is the importance of asking good questions that allow you to fully understand what the prospect wants.

The Perfect Sales Pro will seek to understand the preliminary buying factors that have the greatest effect of gaining your target market's attention, and use those factors in (or near) your introduction, whether you are selling directly, writing sales letters, giving presentations, etc. Transition from preliminary buying factors to primary buying factors. Then close (p.s. you may need more than one preliminary or primary buying factor before closing).

Ask a lot of questions that cause the prospect to become more and more specific about his internalization of his situation. Such questions could begin with:

- What's important to you about…?
- Why is that important to you…?
- What would cause you to…?
- What's the <u>one</u> thing…?
- What would happen if…?
- If you could… ?
- What would be…?
- What causes you to…?

## Buying Criteria

Often referred to as secondary buying factors, or optional buying factors, buying or purchase criteria are the standards and features that help the prospect to evaluate a product and lead them to the purchasing of one product over another similar product (or one that fulfills the same goals, needs or desires). This could include price, quality, location, the manufacturer of the product, the size, the shape, the packaging, the appearance, and so on.

For most customers, many of these criteria are optional. It is thus important to determine the importance of the prospect's list of criteria. Does the prospect really need a four-door sedan, or will a two-door do just fine? Does the prospect really need a bigger widget, or will the smaller one perform the same job? Directly ask the prospect what criteria he has in his new product, and follow up by seeking to understand which of these criteria are a necessity, and on which of them he is more flexible. Often, prospects will complety forgo one set of criteria, in order to fulfill another.

## Buying Reluctance

Zig Ziglar suggests that all buyer reasons for not making the purchase can be summarized into five main categories: No money, no hurry, no need, no desire, and no trust. Either they have no money; they are not in a hurry; they have no need for the item; they have no desire for the item; or they do not trust the item, salesperson or company.

Often, these five reasons can be overcome by applying a different perspective on the situation, or by making the buyer aware of facts that he either may not have been aware of, or simply may not have previously considered. Let's look at one of these as an example: No hurry - By letting he buyer know that a product is exclusively available for a limited time, and will NEVER be available again, it eliminates the "no hurry" reasoning. If the prospect wants, or thinks he may later want, the product, he must buy NOW! The prospect is moved from "no hurry" to "must buy now".

You can also use different methods to change the degree to which a prospect "wants" your product (desire). You do this by helping the prospect see the "need" for your product; providing information that sheds new light on his situation or upcoming situation; or by matching his future desires (hope) to the benefits (and/or advantages) of the product. In the early days of the internet, when most companies were still skeptic about the development and future existent of the internet, search engines helped companies see how the internet was going to be around for a long time, and if they wanted to get ahead of their competition – They needed to begin advertising online immediately! Last on the bandwagon would be last to succeed! Effectively, search engines created a need in the mind of prospects, a need they may not have otherwise realized.

You can have all the right things in place, all the right benefits, all the right influences provoked, and give the prospect all the right reasons to buy... Still there will be some that won't buy. I know what you're thinking right now... Why wouldn't they?... There are reasons that don't make logical sense... Reasons that just are, because of the nature of people in general. These include: Human inertia (a person's desire to avoid change and continue doing what they have been doing); Comfort Zone (people get comfortable where they are); the desire to avoid emotional stress; and the fear of making a bad decision.

 Fear, by the way, is the largest single contributor to decision-making. Fear of appearing unintelligent... Fear of making a bad decision... Fear of loss! People are driven by fear more than any other single factor. If you could do one thing to dramatically improve your sales, it would be to learn how to instill fear in the mind of your prospects, and drive that fear to an emotional peak!

In my twenties, I sold eaves trough protection. I would focus heavily on those houses that showed signs of moisture damage just below the eaves trough, and then approach the home-owners (attempting to speak directly to the woman of the house), and I would introduce facts that they may not have been aware of… "You may not be aware…" I would say… "But moisture in you fascia is a common entry point for spiders. You see, they like damp areas, and once they enter into the fascia, the cracks in the wood allow them direct entry into your home". The woman of the home was usually very responsive to this true statement.

## Decision Making

So how do buyers make that final decision - To buy or not to buy? As you have noticed, between the differences in personality type, influences, personal preferences, the buying process, buying factors and additional factors causing reluctance - A single buying decision can be a very complicated process... And it usually all happens in a very short period of time.

The final decision, whether to go ahead with the purchase or not, happens within a split second. Like a trigger that gets switched inside the brain, telling the buyer what to do. Some of the processes that go on inside the brain include assessing the pros and cons (often referred to as a cost / benefit ratio analysis); prioritizing what's most important to them; analyzing the potential opportunities and losses that may occur from the decision; and evaluating potential repercussions of a decision. Once again, the brain is so powerful that it usually makes these assessments within a fraction of a second. For more costly items, however, the decision making is usually prolonged and a more in-depth analysis is usually performed, as people are generally afraid to make a bad decision.

What's important here, is to realize the way in which time, logic, and emotion play their part in the decision making process. To put it simply, in the average sale, logic and emotion are like two parts of a scale... As one goes up, the other comes down. Remember earlier we said that buying decisions are made emotionally, and are justified with logic... That means that you have to play on the right emotions in order to close the sale. It also means that you have to refrain the prospect from placing too much logic on the final decision (after all, chances are he really does not need whatever it is that you're selling).

Time is a factor that plays in the prospect's favor. The more time the prospect is given to make the decision, the more time he has to calm his inner-emotions and place more logic on the final decision... Which could mean realizing he doesn't need your product, or it could mean realizing that he should look into competitive offers.

## Biases

As intelligent beings, people try to continuously move toward pleasure, and attempt to avoid pain. Therefore, when we make decisions, we try to make the decision that will give us the most benefit or pleasure. Sometimes our decisions do include varying degrees of pain or cost, but the alternative to what we choose is perceived as being more painful or more costly. My perception of any one thing, however, may be different from yours; and my perception of a potential outcome may be different from yours (or anybody else's). This is because we all have different filters within our brain that help us form ideas and concepts about... Well... Everything! These filters, or more specifically, the result of these filters, are called biases.

There are hundreds of biases that have been recognized in psychology. A few important biases include: **1. Confirmation Bias**: People tend to seek evidence that supports the conclusion that they want to have, and attempt to ignore evidence that does not support their pre-established conclusion. Some people are so reluctant to consider evidence against their belief, unless that evidence is extremely overwhelming. **2. Conservatism Bias:** With any topic (an idea, a product, etc.), people generally tend to believe the information that was presented to them regarding that topic, until sufficient evidence to the contrary exists. If prior knowledge exists, and the new information does not match that prior knowledge, people will tend to scrutinize the new information until sufficient evidence is available as proof. ***3. Selective Perception:*** Since people receive millions of bits of information every second, our minds are programmed to filter out information that it believes is not important. Only information which appears important is brought to our consciousness. This filter is called selective perception. The degree or variance as to what is considered important and what is not, is different from person to person.

What this all means is that you should try to help your prospects establish a conclusion by means of emotion, and then providing them with evidence (logic) to support that conclusion. With some products, prospects will have already established their own conclusion prior to your involvement - In order to sway these prospects to your point of view, you will need to provide support or evidence that is sufficient enough to change their point of view. Such evidence may include references to extensive change, emotionally dramatic details, or shocking information,

With regards to information, begin by understanding what the prospect already knows about your product. Be prepared for the types of questions your prospect may ask, and the types of questions they may think about, but never really ask. Have these questions answered and available for you prospects, of course, skewed to present your strengths. People are less likely to go out looking for evidence when the evidence they seek is presented to them. They'll also tend to believe whatever information you give them unless they have experience or information to the contrary. One of the most frequent questions that I came across in my days is "how does that compare to other available sources?", essentially, prospects often want to know if they can get a better deal someone else... So have competitor information pre-prepared for your prospects!

Through selective perception, people tend to ignore what is normal, usual or common; and pay greater attention that which is extra-ordinary or comparatively different. The thing about objects of difference, is that everybody wants them... This is because people like to feel special, and they can achieve this by owning something that no-body else has *(Part of "the scarcity principle")*. These are very important principles... If you're preparing marketing or advertising material, you can gain people's attention quickly by making your ad "different". If you're giving a speech or presentation, you can get your audience's attention by doing something out-of-the-ordinary. If you're selling, you get people to consider your offer in greater depth by offering something of value that they cannot get anywhere else.

You can learn more about consumer psychology in The Master Sales Manual, and subsequent books.

# Concept #3

## Improve Your Communication

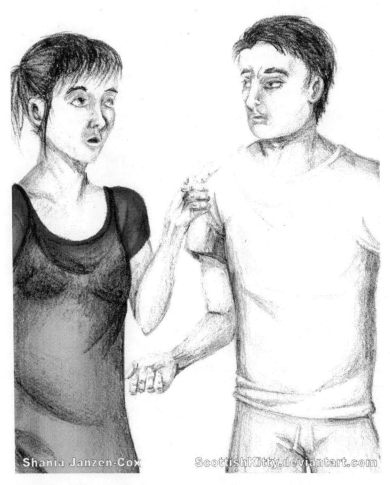

$\mathcal{G}$ood communication skills are not enough. You need to have great communication skills to be the Perfect Sales Pro. That doesn't mean that you just need to improve the way that you talk, and the words that you use... Great communication means that you must improve your speaking skills and listening skills, but also means that you have improve your writing abilities as well as your use and understanding of non-verbal communication and body language.

Communication, regardless of what form it takes, should follow 7 key requirements known as the 7 C's of effective communication. It should be clear, concise, concrete, correct, coherent, complete, and courteous.

## Developing Small Talk

Small talk is often the part that people have the most trouble with. Why? Because they are afraid of being rejecting after initially engaging a stranger. This is also true for salespeople who perform any form of cold-calling - whether by phone, or in-person. Most selling situations, however, require you to get out of your comfort zone and approach people. The key to over-coming this fear is very simple, just do it! The more you learn to face rejection, the more you learn to just move on. Timing could be of some importance depending on the particular situation.

The one most important aspect of developing small talk is to gain the other person's attention. Of course, you want to do this in a courteous and respectful manner. Being abrupt, impolite or offensive with someone will certainly disfavor any additional or future conversation. You can gain people's attention in a variety of ways, including: Gaining eye contact; asking simple questions that are easy to answer; and directing conversation toward the other person's self-interest (those things that THEY are interested in). I often get asked "When establishing small-talk with a stranger, how do you know what _they_ are interested in?"... In response, I answer "I simply observe them, and look for things such as items they may be holding, topics they may be talking about, or anything that sets them apart from others in the immediate vicinity". For example, if I see a businessman sitting in a coffee shop reviewing papers, I may make a comment or ask a question about his paperwork, his attire, how busy he appears, or so on. Often, after having made an initial remark, I would leave a momentary break before re-engaging in conversation, simply to allow that conversation to appear more spontaneous and less pre-planned.

One of the subtle keys of developing small talk is to establish common-ground. This can be anything that causes either a simple agreement on a topic, or a mutual understanding. By establishing common-ground, you are creating the perception that you understand the prospect (or whomever you are creating small-talk with) and that you are similar. Remember that people like people who are just like them.

## Building Rapport

Rapport is developed when the prospect likes you and trusts you. The fastest way to gain this type of rapport is to be just like them. When we recognize someone as being alike or similar to ourselves, we feel that we understand them on a profound level. The goal is to get them to think, either consciously or unconsciously "This person is just like me, and I like and trust myself, therefore, I must also like and trust this person".

 Verbally, you can gain rapport by talking at the same pace as the other person, talking at the same volume, using the same inflection, using the same key words and sentences, and so on. You can also mimic their body language, gestures, and other non-verbal cues. Be cautious, however, that the other person does not recognize you doing this intentionally, as they may become offended that you are mimicking them. With large and more prominent gestures, you may consider leaving a 3-4 second intermission before copying the other person's gestures. Small gestures are very hard to copy if you are untrained, and may take practice but can also yield the greatest results.

I often receive the same reaction from reps that I've trained in this regard, they say "isn't that deception? ", or "that's not natural?". Remember, however, that persuasion of any type (including sales) requires the ability to adapt to circumstances. Let's take a look at an example: Would you talk the same way to your grandma, as you would talk to your friends? Probably not! Would you act the same way at a football game that you would act in a lawyer's office? Probably not! So I rest my case, adaption is key, everywhere... It's called having a "flexible personality".

## Specificity

Probably the biggest issue in human communication, is that people are not specific about what they want to say.

Communication is full of ambiguity and non-specific communication that results in confusion and misunderstanding.

While there are times when you may want to confuse people in order to achieve a particular goal, you should generally to aim to be as specific as possible in your communication. This is a trait of the perfect communicator.

First... Don't talk more than you need to. In the movie "Ocean's Eleven", Rusty says to Livingston "Don't use seven words when four will do". People often have a tendency to continue talking long after they've concluded their point. In sales, it is commonly understood that many salespeople lose the sale because they talk too much. Even I find myself practicing restraint, especially during emotional phases.

Second... Understand that, as people, we normally communicate in terms of thoughts and ideas - We have an idea, and we translate that idea into words. It is thus important to turn those thoughts and ideas into precise words that are aimed at achieving a goal. The word "house" for example, has a different implication then the word "home" (a house is a structure; while a home is where family is)... The word "child" has a different meaning to most people, then the word "kid" (child relates to closeness and innocence, while "kid" simply refers to person who is not an adult, and could be of any age between 1 week and twenty years.) - Think about your choice of words, and don't use words that have no purpose. It is up to you to decide what goal you want to achieve, and then choose the words and phrases that are best suited to achieve that goal.

This means that we don't just talk because we have something to say, but rather because we want to get the other person to react in a specific way, or to hold certain thoughts, beliefs or understanding. There are methods of performing this, all outlined in my next book: *The Master Sales Manual*.

## Listening

Listening is one of those communication skills that most people take for granted. Would you assume that when you listen to someone speak, you must have heard what they are saying? Most people would. The intent that one person has in the listening process, however, changes what we hear and how we understand it. As mentioned in the previous chapter, the brain filters all the information that we receive to prevent itself from overloading. This filtering process, often referred to as "sensory gating", is prevalent in our listening process depending on the intent that we have when we engage in listening... And we don't always have the same intent! Sometimes people listen because they seek to hear specific information; sometimes we listen because they want to know that you agree with them; sometimes we listen only to the main ideas that are portrayed and disregard specific content; and still other times we listen only to aid in developing the relationship, and thus only focus on key information needed to do so. There are also a myriad of other reasons for listening, such as empathy, emotional reflection and casual listening, which is what we do most of the time.

It's important to remember that listening problems happen, not only in your listening abilities, but also in the listening of your prospects, customers and... Well... Everybody. So if you don't grasp everything that is being said, and they don't grasp everything that is being said, communication becomes quite skewed.

The perfect listener, will be able to grasp or understand beyond the mere listening process. The speed at which a person speaks, the tone of their voice, the gestures they use and the movement of their eyes, are but small examples of the subtleties of human communication that are almost always overlooked. Learn to recognize these nuances and their meanings under context.

In addition to lack of effective listening skills, there are also many things that can act as obstacles, preventing effective listening. Problems in one's ability to listen; attending problems such as distractions; understanding or comprehension issues; memory errors; incorrect interpretations and issues that arise in evaluating what is important and what is not. You can now see the importance of specificity. Learn to recognize the issues surrounding your prospect's ability to listen attentively, and adjust your presentation accordingly. This means you may need to speak slower for some people, louder for others, and possibly repeat key areas of the presentation several times, or even use cues to remind them of those key factors that you have presented.

## Writing

The first consideration in effective writing is to ensure that you have a good grasp on the basics. Review your understanding of the basic parts of a speech, such as how to effectively use adverbs and adjectives (which by the way are very powerful in spoken and written communication); how to use punctuation correctly; and what are the parts of whichever type of documents you intend to work with. Remember that people are always judging you, every second of your life, and in everything you do, and poorly written or structured material may result in a lack of trust, both in you, and in your words.

Below we will discuss only a few of the many techniques and methods of making your literary material more interesting...

**Narrative Mode**

Narrative mode is the way in which you present what you have to say. It is much more useful in written communication, although may be used in spoken language also. There are three aspects of narrative mode that are important: ***1. Narrative Mode*** - The point of view by which the information is being told - whether that point of view is that of yourself involved in the information (first person); or whether you're are talking to your reader as if they are involved (second person); or whether you present the information as an observer, observing someone else (third party). **2. *Narrative voice*** - describes how the information is told. This is important because it gives the reader some indication as to where the material comes from. Were you there? Did you experience the situation, or were you an observer? You may be talking to yourself, telling about past events or imposing your point of view of the information that you present. This may be the difference between using words such as "I did it" and "I saw it happen" or "I was told that it happened". The reader's perception of the information may be different in each case.

 Too many people use narrative voice from the view of a first person – That is, using the word "I" throughout the material. Self-Interest or personal ego tend to work their way into written communication the way it does spoken communication. Consider structuring your writing differently – Instead of writing "I wrote this book for salespeople", write "Dan wrote this book for salespeople"; or perhaps switch to passive voice "This book was written for salespeople".

**Active and Passive Voice**

Active and passive voice refer to whether or not the main subject of your material is the performing an action, or whether someone or something else is acting upon it. It is the difference between saying "you have only learned a portion of the skills you need" (known as active voice); or saying "Only a portion of the skills you need have been learned" (known as passive voice). The subject of these statements, of course, is "you". Another example would be… "The buyer pulled out his wallet and paid for the purchase" (active voice); or "The purchase was paid when the buyer pulled out his wallet (passive voice)".

Active voice is recognized as being more dynamic and exciting, however, there may be times when dynamic and exciting is not preferred, and thus passive voice is the best to use in these circumstances.

**Mood Alteration**

When you write, it is important to pay attention to the mood that you are portraying in your choice of, and presentation of, the words and sentence you use. Are you asking questions? Giving orders? Or thinking out loud? Consider how each of these will affect the reader. You can change the mood of the reader by your choice of words, by the way words are arranged in a sentence, and by the punctuation used.

To clarify, consider the difference between the following sentences: 1. Go grab me another hammer! 2. Can you go grab me another hammer? 3. Would you go grab me another hammer please? 4. I wish you would go grab me another hammer. 5. I wish he would just go grab me another hammer!

You can easily see how each of these sentences portrays a different mood from the point of the speaker. From angry to inquisitive to self-thinking.

Take careful consideration of the mood alteration used in your sales letters, stories, advertising, and other marketing.

## Transitions

Transitions help two parts of a sentence, two sentences, or two paragraphs, connect in a smooth way. Think about the way in which two sections of your writing will be connected together. These two sections may separate ideas or they may separate a question and an answer or possibly different forms of writing (i.e. different narrative modes, mood alterations etc.)... You may have several parts within a story or within a document that can be connected through the use of effective transitions.

Some methods of creating effective transitions include using words that show similarity, dissimilarity or contradiction, logical conclusions, or any other such patterns. For example, if I was writing a letter to my boss, asking for a raise, I may begin my letter by referring to all of the good work that I've done, and then transitioning to how much over time that I've been working - I may use a transitional phrase such as "In addition to my hard work...". I may then go directly into asking for the raise using a transitional phrase such as "With all this in mind" (i.e. with all this in mind, you should deeply consider my request for a raise). You could, of course, forgo all elegance and directly ask for the raise, but that just wouldn't have the same effect!

The perfect writer will preplan any written material, and review it carefully prior to sending it out to a prospect or audience. Ensure that all parts mentioned above are coming across in the desired manner. Pay special attention to how people will feel when they read your material!

## Non-Verbal Communication

Often mistakenly confused as body-language, non-verbal communication includes body-language as well as a variety of other forms of non-verbal communication. This includes proxemic communication, gestures, gesture-clusters, micro-gestures and facial signals, head gestures, and minor vocal sounds (umms, ahhhs, etc).

The Perfect Sales Pro will have a good grasp of non-verbal communication and how it can help you to understand what people are saying, when they aren't saying everything. This can also help build rapport because people come to realize that you understand them, and when people believe you understand them, they tend to want to connect with you on a deeper level.

**Proxemic Communication**

Actually referred to as "proxemics", this is the communication that is portrayed by your distance to other people. Generally speaking, the closer we get to others, the more we communicate on a personal level. The further we are from someone, the less personal we communicate. Directly touching someone is generally considered interpersonal communication. We also communicate a message by the length of time in which we remain within a particular proximity to others – The longer we remain within a close proximity, the more powerful the message becomes. These messages we portray have an effect on the way in which we are perceived by others.

Imagine for a moment, that you meet up with a business partner for the first time. Perhaps you recently started doing business together and have only spoken on the phone until this moment. Your initial greeting begins with a handshake. Your handshake will portray a different message to your partner depending on whether you use one hand or two (less contact, or more contact). The distance that you stand apart from your partner during the handshake will also leave a different impression, as well as your distance immediately after the handshake.

The above was just one example of how proxemics can make a difference. The Perfect Sales Pro will consciously think about the messages that he is sending through proxemic communication. Consider your three most common situations in which proxemics may be important, and design the message you would wish to portray. As in the example above, also consider the three most common types of people (i.e. customers, business partners, friends, etc.) whom you shake hands with, and prepare your handshakes in advance to ensure that you are always sending the message you want to send.

**Body Language**

When reading body language, it is important not only to consider the individual gestures that a person is making, but also to consider how several gestures may be working together – These are called "gesture clusters". It is also important to understand the emotion that is being conveyed through one's use of their body-language, as well as the situation or context.

There are thousands of gestures that can be made with the body, and there are twice as many gesture clusters. There are, however, some general guidelines that may help in simplifying them: ***1. Open vs. Closed***: When people use open gestures, they are inviting others into their space. They are generally open-minded and have nothing to hide. Causing someone to place themselves into an open gesture can have similar effects on the mind, so if you want someone to be more open minded - make sure they position themselves more openly. When people use closed body language, they usually either trying to create a barrier between themselves and the world around them, or shut themselves off from their surroundings in some way. ***2. High vs. Low:*** People who try to place themselves above others, or otherwise place themselves in a high position, are most likely showing some form of dominance, superiority or control. This includes the subtle things such as the raising of one's head, the position of one's hand during a handshake, the posture of one's body, and so on. When people place themselves in a lower position in comparison to others, they are being submissive, humble or portraying inferiority. ***2. Close vs. Distant:*** As mentioned earlier, people who try to get close to you are attempting to be more personal. However, when people distance themselves from you, they are trying to become less personal.

The Perfect Sales Pro will be conscientious of the body language that others use, as well as his own. Recognize that the position of your body changes your frame of mind, and use this information to put people into the frame of mind that you desire them to be in.

### Facial Expressions

Understanding facial expressions beyond the common basics is rather difficult without training. Emotions are primarily expressive in the facial region of the eyes and mouth, and it is here that most micro-expressions are prominent. Micro-expressions are small and subtle movements that are usually involuntary, meaning they happen without our conscious involvement.

If you were planning on teaching yourself how to recognize facial expressions, you could, to some degree of effectiveness, mimic some facial expression of another individual, and then ask yourself how you would be feeling if you were forming such a facial expression for real. Facial expressions are universal, which means the feelings that one person would feel performing certain expressions, is most likely the same feelings that another person would feel if they were performing the same expression. The next step would be simply to memorize the complexities of that particular expression.

# Handshakes

Handshakes are one of the most common interactions between two people - They are performed when meeting people, greeting people, leaving people, offering congratulations and completing agreements. A simple handshake can tell a lot about a person. Handshakes require that each person enter into the other person's personal space. Some people use this as a way of building relationships, while others try to stray away from handshakes, even though it is a customary ritual. Some use handshakes as a show of superiority, while others don't use handshakes consciously at all.

Individual personalities are portrayed by the way we shake another person's hand. Some guidelines are as follows: *1. Rigid vs. Soft Handshakes:* Rigid handshakes are used by those who are attempting to show strength, power, dominance or superiority. Soft handshakes are used by those who express themselves as timid, weak, subordinate or feminine. *2. Open vs. Closed Handshakes:* When a person initiates their handshake with wide or open body language, they are presenting themselves as being open, honest, transparent and friendly. Closed body language in during a handshake is symbolic of secrecy, closing oneself off from the other, and unfriendliness. This includes the degree to which the hand is opened or closed during the handshake itself. *3. Quick vs. Long Handshakes:* People who are quick in their handshakes are generally attempting to return to their personal space as soon as possible. This may be a show of masculinity, or it may be in attempt to close oneself off (emotionally) from the other person. Long handshakes, however, are a sign of openness and an attempt to develop strong relationships. Be cautious though, as long-handshakes may be just as deceitful as quick handshakes... Politicians use long handshakes (often using both hands) as part of an attempt to gain trust and friendship… And we all know we can trust politicians, right!?

Handshakes have become so important amongst business professionals that hundreds of different types of handshakes have been identified and given names. Some of the most popular are: ***1. The Dead Fish:*** Mainly used by women, this handshake is characterized by the seemingly boneless hand that extends with no pressure, as the four fingers droop downward, either vertically or horizontally. ***2. The Dominator:*** This handshake is an attempt to show the receiver who is in power by gaining higher ground (in terms of the hands). This is performed by immediately pressing downward with the palm facing to the ground (may vary in degrees), which forces the other person's palm to face upward... ***3. The Glove:*** Also known as the politician's handshake, because politicians are well known for their misleading attempt to show honesty and friendship. In this handshake, one hand grasps the receiver's hand in a level position, while the other hand grasps the back of the hand or wrist in a show of closeness.

**The Dead Fish     The Dominator     The Glove**

The Perfect Sales Pro understands that "people like people who are just like them". This applies to handshakes, just as well as it does to everything else. The Perfect Sales Pro will approach every handshake opportunity with an open attitude... Let the other person extend their arm first (even if only by a split second). Watch carefully how people extend their arms to initiate a handshake - Are they extending their arms openly, or more closely toward the body, quickly or slowly, etc. Then extend yours in the same manner. Wait for the other person to begin squeezing your hand, and use the same mannerism - The same firmness, the same pressure - Essentially, let them lead, and you follow, throughout the handshaking process. Now, at least in this regard, they will perceive you as being just like them. Instant rapport.

## Eye Gestures

The secret is in the eyes. William Shakespeare once said "The eyes are the windows to the soul". The eyes are one of the few parts of the person's expression that is completely controlled by unconscious emotion. We cannot hide the expressions of the eyes, they just happen... Though sometimes we notice our eye gestures quickly after they occur and try to hide them by restoring a straight-face.

There are eight basic directions in which the eyes can move, and each of these gives a certain insight into the consumer mind. Here, we will cover the four most basic principles that apply to eye gestures: ***1. Looking Up:*** When people look upward, they are creating images in their mind. ***2. Looking Down:*** When people look down, they are generally attempting to access inner emotions, unless they are looking straight down which is a display of hiding or shying away from others. ***3. Looking To The Left and Right:*** Looking to the right refers to searching within oneself, possibly creating some new feelings or imagery (depending on if they are looking down or up); and looking to the left the person is accessing memory. Looking directly to the left means the person is accessing sounds that have previously been heard; while looking directly to the right means the person is constructing new sounds.

So what? You may ask...Why do I need to pay attention to people's eye gestures? Watching eye gestures bring a new depth of understanding your prospects to the table. It allows you to gain further insight as to whether people are speaking with deep emotion (eyes down), or speaking from experience (eyes toward the left), or if they are imagining themselves using your product (eyes up and toward the right). It can also let you know when people are lying to you or telling the truth.

You can learn more about communication skills in The Master Sales Manual, and subsequent books.

# Concept #4
## Market Yourself

$\mathcal{R}$egardless of what type of sales you ae in (with some exceptions), you should be looking for ways to market yourself, and brand yourself in an appropriate manner. There are several books available on topics such as self-marketing, guerilla marketing, and branding. The specific channels used may be different for each individual depending on the type of sales they are involved in, the company they work with and the products or services they represent.

## Have A Plan

The first step in self-marketing is to develop a plan. This may take 30 seconds or 30 days depending on the complexity of your plan. Complex plans are not always necessary, and you may want to consider how deeply you are involved in the total sales and marketing process.

You may also want to create a separate plan just for your sales cycle. This should include information about the marketplace, the manner in which you plan to generate leads (prospects), as well as how you plan to turn each lead into a sale or customer. Finally, and especially important in today's age, you want to plan out how you are going to provide after-sale support - this could be a simple phone call on a timely basis just to see how things are going, and could lead into referrals and other forms of additional business - People appreciate knowing that you care.

## Understanding The Sales Cycle.

The sales cycle, often referred to as the sales funnel, is a step by step process in which sales are generated. It includes seven basic steps that should be followed in order. They are *1. Prospecting:* Often referred to as lead-generation, prospecting involves finding people who may have an interest in your offer. You begin with a list of "leads" (potential prospects), and you will contact each lead to determine which of these could possibly be interested in your offer. *2. Qualifying:* You should set the criteria by which you believe a prospect would be suitable for your product, or your product would be suitable for a prospect, and ask a series of questions to qualify each prospect (i.e. do they have enough money to purchase the offer?). *3. Setting The Appointment:* The appointment is where you present your offer. This may be set at a later point in time, or it may be immediate (combined with the prospecting phase). If you are cold-calling, or going door-to-door, you may get an immediate appointment or opportunity to present your offer with the prospect on the phone or at the door – So be ready and prepared to present ahead of time. *4. Presenting:* Go to or get involved in the appointment, and present your offer. *5. Selling:* Selling involves asking question, persuading, handling objections, negotiating and performing trial closes. Each of these steps may vary in length depending on circumstances. *6. Close The Sale:* Complete the transaction, get the contract signed or make an exchange of money for a product or service. *7. Get Referrals:* Ask for referrals or prospects of any other person they may know who could use your product or service.

## Understand Your Environment

To be the Perfect Sales Pro, you must know your environment. You don't want to try selling an item that is out of date, or charge twice as much for your item as your competitors, or sell in a way which is against legal means. For example: At the time of writing this book, Canada is launching its official anti-spam law of 2014.

There are a series of market analysis formulas that may be used to research your environment, but the most important areas to consider are **1.** A comparison of your (total) offer and that of the competition; **2.** Your strengths and weaknesses; **3.** An analysis of opportunities to gain market share, and the threats involved in doing so (there may be several ways to do this, so analyze them all).

## Target Marketing

I like to call this target-prospecting: Target marketing is about choosing the prospects that are best suited for your offer. Sure... you could just sell to everybody... If you think everybody will buy from you. It is more likely, however, that there is a certain type of prospect that will be more ready buy... and these prospects will have similar characteristics. Consider some of the following: **1. Demographics:** Where do your prospect's live? How old are they? Are they male or female? What ethnicity are they?

How much money do they make? **2. Psychographics:** What values do your prospects have? What opinions do they have on matters related to your offer? What interests do they have? What do they do on their leisure time? What kind of lifestyle do they hold? What's important to them?  **3. Behavioral Characteristics:**  How do your prospects behave under defined conditions? (You'll have to define the conditions that are relevant to your offer and selling process).  How loyal are they?  What do draws them in and what do they prefer to stay away from?  Why would they buy one item over another?

 Once you have a better understanding of your target market, you can use this knowledge to refine your sales, marketing and advertising efforts.  All of your efforts should be tailored, as specifically as possible, to your target market.  For example: If you know that your target market works from 9am - 5pm, don't cold call them in the middle of the day.  If their income is not substantial, don't offer high-ticket items.

 If your company's marketing department does any form of targeted marketing or advertising, you may want to consult with them

## Prospecting

You could just present your offer to every Joe who comes along, but the chances of everybody wanting your product or service is slim to none. If this is the method you use… I can guarantee you are wasting a lot of your time.

Prospecting is about finding those people (or companies, or groups, etc.) who are most likely to buy your product, allowing you to sell more with less effort.  The perfect prospect, therefore, would include those people who are either already seeking what you have to offer (at your price, location, etc.); or who is already seeking a solution that your product will solve, and simply is not aware of your offer.

If there were an abundance of perfect prospects, salespeople would quickly be replaced with order-takers, and marketing departments would simply focus all of their marketing directly to those perfect prospects. It is much more likely that very few perfect prospects exist, and it then becomes the salesperson's responsibility to spend his efforts wisely by focusing on those prospects who are the best <u>possible</u> match. Sales, thus, becomes a matter of finding the right people to sell to, and then sell the right thing to the people you find.

**Qualifying The Prospect**

Before you can move forward and sell your offer to the prospect, you need to make sure that the prospect is able to buy, wants to buy, and is going to make a purchase soon. Some things to inquire about are: ***1. Authority:*** Confirm the prospect has the authority to buy. ***2. Buying Process:*** Try to understand the prospect's buying process. ***3. Criteria:*** Ask what criteria the prospect needs to fulfill, and what criteria will sway his decision to a positive one. ***4. Estimated Purchase Date:*** Find out what the estimated purchase date would be (anything over one year should not be qualified). ***5. Budget:*** Ensure that they have the budget to make the purchase, or provide alternatives that are more suitable for their budget. ***6. Interest:*** Secure their interest in buying your product (as oppose to alternatives). Make sure they not only want to buy now, but will be happy with their purchase once they get it home.

**Classifying The Prospect**

Not all prospects are created equal, so once we qualify someone as a prospect, we must classify them in order of importance. This helps us to know which prospects deserve most of our time, and which prospects do not.

The best way to classify your prospects is to create a simple scale, and place each prospect on that scale in order of their readiness to buy. You can simply create a scale of 1 to 5, where one represents those ready to buy, and 5 represents those who are not likely to buy in the next year; or use a scale such as hot, warm, cool and cold.

## Finding Prospects

There are two types of methods used to find prospect: "Push methods", in which you reach out to potential prospects; and "pull methods", in which you try to get prospect's to come to you. Push methods include such tactics as email, sales letters, cold-calling, etc. Pull methods are performed by placing some form of attractive marketing or advertising in key areas, that persuade the viewer to contact you - those prospects who reach out to you are generally easier to sell to, as they are contacting you with some level of pre-established interest or some degree of openness regarding your offer.

Some methods of finding prospects include: **1.** Socializing; **2.** Marketing and advertising; **3.** Directories and other sources; **4.** Reaching out to similar types of people; **5.** Connecting with people within targeted groups.

## Advertising

The Perfect Sales Pro should have an understanding of basic marketing and advertising, and will attempt to use at least some of those principles in everyday communication, irrespective of whether or not he has any direct involvement in marketing and advertising of the company or product. Many of these ideas and principles can be used in the creation of business cards, flyers and the such; while others can be used in daily communication such as emails, sales letters and so on.

**Call To Action**

Every piece of marketing or advertising that you send out should give people some direction or indication of what to do next. Most people want to be told what to do... Not to say that people cannot think for themselves, but often, if you do not tell them what to do next, they will not consider doing it on their own. A "call to action" is just that... It is a suggestive command given to the viewer or audience of a marketing or advertising piece, telling them what to do next.

A call to action may be anything that you want the prospect to do after having viewed your ad or listened to your offer. This may be to contact you via phone or email; or it may be to go online and complete the purchase.

Depending on your marketing strategy, you may not want the prospect to contact you right away... You might want to direct them to another form of marketing to aid in driving their desire to a higher peak... For example: You may write a sales letter that invites the prospect to visit your website. Your website, in turn, may invite them receive a free Audio CD. Once they receive that, the Audio CD may then direct them to call you for more content. Of course... That's all in the realm of marketing, which is not the real focus of this book.

## Benefits

Make sure that any marketing or advertising also focuses on the benefits that your offer will bring to the prospect. You can't expect to sell anything until you first establish value. You must be able to gain the prospect's interest in what your ad is saying, in order to compel him to follow through with your call to action. Your statement of benefits should be clear and concise so that your target market does not have to work too hard to understand why they should buy. Keep both your USP and ESP in mind here (see chapter 6).

## Themes

If you are putting out multiple advertising (which you should be doing anyway), consider creating a theme, such as a repetition or a succession of ideas that work in coordination with each other. One my favorite themes was used by the mega battery company Energizer, in which they used a repeated character or mascot (the Energizer Bunny) who outlasted the competitive batteries (which is what people <u>want</u> when they buy batteries - a longer lasting battery!).

Themes can also be used as a method of branding. Branding involves establishing a set of defined characteristics and properties that identify and distinguish you, your product and / or your company from the competition. This can include the images you use; the characters (or type of characters) that represent you; the images you use; the logos you use; and just about anything else you can think of. When a prospect or customer (or a potential prospect or customer) comes into contact with those defined characteristics and properties, he should immediately identify them as being associated to you, your product and / or your company (at least once you become more popular). This book is branded as a Master Sales Manual series of books, with the following logo or ribbon (to the right):

## Colors

Everything that is presented to our senses, changes the way we think, feel and behave. If you were a computer, every aspect of every sound, every image, every smell and every feeling would be considered input. All this input affects us in one way or another, sometimes drastically, and sometimes in a more subtle manner. Since people think largely by association, we tend to view colors by associating them with the most common objects or images that are made of each color... For example, when we think of green, we are likely to think of money (at least if you live in North America). Every color also presents a contrasting effect: Some people, when they think of the color green, will most immediately think of nature (grass, trees, herbs, etc.). With this being said, it become especially important to consider how you are using each color, as every color can provide both a positive and a negative effect on one's perception. Let's take a look at another color.... say... Red. Red can give the implication of blood, death or pain... Red can also give the perception of passion and sex appeal.

The effect that colors present becomes more and more appealing when two or more colors are combined together. The manner in which they contrast and the over-all perception of the combined colors can be so strong as to allow us to imagine things that aren't really there... Several shades of brown mixed with a little black, for instance, can give the impression of rugged terrain. You wouldn't want to use these colors in your letter-head if you were trying to sell fashion clothing. Consider the colors you use and the effect they are having on your target audience.

**Advertising Location**

Don't just place your ads anywhere. The best place for your ads, is exactly where your target market is going to be. This means before you place your ads, you must have first defined a target market (who is most likely to buy your product). If you can define, not just where your target market may be, but rather where your target market will spend <u>most</u> of their time, this would be the optimal place for your ads.

## Internet Marketing

The internet has changed the world of sales and marketing alike. Now, you can reach more people, communicate with the world, and share your marketing and advertising with everybody. That doesn't necessarily mean you should! Target marketing should still be the focus of your sales... however, it now becomes easier to reach other markets as well.

**Call To Action**

Marketing on the internet is, essentially, no different than marketing anywhere else. Certainly, you may also want to consider all of the previously mentioned lessons on color-psychology, themes, branding, etc. Above all, however, you want to ensure that every piece of marketing or advertising that you release, includes a call-to action. This includes your web-pages, blogs, email, etc. I have re-written my email signature as a mini-ad that directs people to my website to buy my next book.

## Links

Internet marketing is all about spreading the word to a larger audience, geographically speaking, and driving traffic (Hoards of people who are interested in your topic or offer) to your door - Whether that be a website, a blog, an online store, your personal contact information, or wherever you would like that traffic to go to. This means you must be able to spread the word in as many places as possible, and direct people to where you want them to be, or what you want them to do... You do this by creating links from as many other places on the internet as possible (this is called "link-building").

This is where we go back to our target marketing. If you're selling houses for instance... You can put links to your email address on other types of pages that are associated to buying a house. If you know your target market well enough, you don't have to limit yourself to websites that are strictly designed to sell houses... Let's assume your target market is a higher end class of people, with an income range of about $70,000 per person, who are married and both parties in the marriage are employed (meaning the household income is about $140,000). This type of target market may not only have interests in buying houses, but may also buy boats, and go on vacation at least once a year - You may want to find ways of creating links on those types of pages and websites also, possibly with a small written (or pictorial) advertisement.

Consider not only your target market, but those people, groups or companies that may directly or indirectly influence your target market (called "Influencers").

**Social Media**

In today's age, you can't speak of self-marketing on the internet without speaking of social media. The idea of social media is not new, it's been around for hundreds of years. The idea is simply one that allows friends, colleagues and like-minded individuals to gather in one spot and communicate on given topics, ranging from personal life, to hobbies, to other special topics – Online social media simply allows that to happen on a greater scale.

With that being said, the simplicity of social media can now be understood. You simply reach out and find other people who are similar to yourself, or who have an interest in the type of product you provide, and share the ideas that surround your product.

Keep in mind, however, that is NOT selling. This is "product recognition" and "relationship development". People, whether online or not, do not like to be bombarded with constant advertising and promotion – Therefore you can't just join social media outlets and continuously repeat your special offers… You need a more subtle approach, appeal to the unconscious and let people think they are making their own decisions to move forward. Some methods of doing this include: ***1. Provide display advertising*** – People will decide to check out your products based on the ad, picture/image or display. ***2. Share information*** – If the information is exciting, fun, interesting or other, people will choose to find out why. ***3. Join discussions*** – You can make subtle remarks that lead people to look into your product, especially where problems or issues are being discussed.

Some of the important forms of social media to look into include:

1. ***Social networking sites*** – This includes sites such as Facebook, Myspace and Linkedin. Be cautious as to what type of people join the different types of social networking sites, and how those types of people correspond to your target market – For example: If your selling business products, you may want to focus more heavily on sites such as LinkedIn, rather than those such as Facebook (more business professionals are on LinkedIn). This is not to say that business professionals do not join Facebook, the type of information shared is different.

2. ***Bookmarking Sites*** – These sites allow you to save and share links to pages across the internet, usually based on some common interest. So if you were surfing the internet and you come across pages you like, you could save it for future reference and then share it with others. Try to get people to share your links (to your products).

3. ***Social News*** – These are sites that allow you to share news about yourself, your products, your company etc. They also allow others to vote on your news articles or ads, and those with the most votes get displayed in a favorable setting.

4. Blogs and micro-blogs – Blogs allow the blog-owner, and usually also allows others who have joined, to post

ideas and content that others can comment on or share their experience. The blog owner will usually start a particular topic of conversation that others can follow or provide some input (very similar to forums, below). Micro-blogs are short updates or posts on recent occurrences (Twitter is currently the most popular micro-blogging website).

5. *Forums* – These are similar to blogs, however, with forums the main content is provided by comments that are given by users who have joined the site or forum.

Again I stress, in social media marketing, subtlety is a key. As mentioned previously, people have been so bombarded by advertising in their everyday lives, that pushing your offer on them here will just turn them away from your offer, which is as simple as the click of a mouse.

You can learn more about self-marketing in The Master Sales Manual, and subsequent books.

# Concept #5

## Prospect For Targets

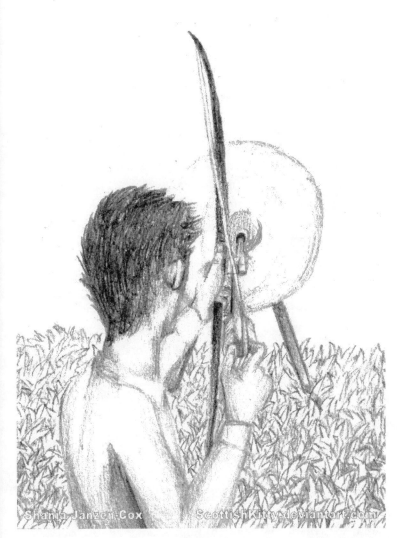

There are essentially three types of prospecting in sales. Of course, that does not include advertising and marketing efforts. What we're talking about here, is strictly in regards to push methods of selling. They are: ***1. Direct Selling:*** This is the art of selling to someone face to face, and includes door-to-door sales, tradeshows, sales appointments. ***2. Telephone Sales:*** This is the art of selling to someone over the telephone, but should be extended to any use of audio-only sales and marketing efforts. ***3. Sales Literature:*** This is the art of selling through the use of the written word, and includes letters, emails, internet pages, articles, books, facsimiles, etc.

A large part of sales, as with marketing, is sending the right message to the right people at the right time. Let's take a look at how we can improve each of the above methods of prospecting...

## Direct Selling

Also known as personal selling or face-to-face selling, direct selling aims to make the sales process as personal as possible. The goal, of course, is to build a strong relationship with the prospect as fast as possible.

In most cases, unless a pre-established appointment has been made, you are probably interrupting the prospect's normal (daily) activity, and thus will want to open your conversation with something interesting, to catch their attention. Keep in mind, that "interesting" means interesting to them, not necessarily to you. This is where the target market research performed in chapter 4 comes in handy. If you have no time to target market beforehand, then at least have some general understand of who you're selling to (the more specific the better).

Make sure that you begin by giving them ample space, so as not to appear too invading. Remember that you first have to build some level of trust before you get too close to people's personal space (most people will want to make sure you are not going to harm them). Leave an open stance or posture, as this will appear less confrontational and do not directly block their available points of exit. Minimize excessive hand gestures as this creates an uncertainty regarding your motives, and when people are unsure of your motives they will not trust you. Keep good eye contact throughout your presentation, but do not constantly stare at people as this also makes people uneasy - simply look away once in a while, perhaps with a mildly emotional or empathetic gesture.

In my personal opinion, every person who is engaged in sales should take some form of acting class. It's important to understand how your actions change your emotions, and vice-versa; and also how your actions and emotions affect the emotions of your prospects, as well as their reception to you. When it comes to prospects (and customers), trust is largely a matter of how much they believe you, and if your actions and emotions are incongruent, lack of trust is the inevitable result.

For best results, practice portrayal of gestures and emotions in front of a mirror, and gauge your own reactions as a viewer. Optionally, you may also ask a friend or family member to assist you by telling you how they feel while you are making a presentation – Let them know ahead of time what type of response you are seeking, and confirm that your presentation is evoking the right emotions and leaving the right impressions.

## Telephone Sales

Before you engage in telephone sales, you should learn to adequately train your voice. You should learn to use inflection, portray emotions at will, control volume and ambiance, and master different tones and vocal styles. Remember that gaining rapport means being similar to your prospect, as well as being liked and trusted.

**Vocal Styles**

In this book, we aim to cover four basic vocal styles, as related to the four interpersonal characteristics covered in chapter 2. Keep in mind, however, that this is an attempt to generalize the most common vocal styles with their associated personalities and may not apply to every individual case.

***1. Commanding:*** Commanding vocal styles are those of the driver type personality. This style can typically be recognize through the use of a low tone of voice coupled with a descending tone at the end of each word, sentence or phrase. Because of the descending tones, words appear to be spoken in a very sharp nature, and spoken quickly.

***2. Monotonous:*** People, who speak with a monotonous style, often taking more frequent breaks between sentences, are likely to portray an analytical personality. The lack of expression and frequent breaks between sentences occur because their minds are occupied analyzing their surroundings or recent occurrences. People using this vocal style will also speak with elongated sentences, as they analyze your response to their speech and consider what to say next. ***3. Energetic:*** Energetic people have energetic vocal styles. This style can be recognized by a higher tone of voice, and the rising of tone or pitch at the end of sentences. They tend to speak rapidly, and their sentences will be short as they will breath inward more frequently in accordance with their higher level of emotion. ***4. Soft and Slow:*** Attempting to mesmerize their listeners, amiable type personalities will often use a soft vocal style. Each word, phrase and sentence will appear stretched out, as if time is never an issue.

In addition to matching vocal styles with each personality, it's important to note that vocal styles can also give some insight as to the particular emotion that a person holds at any given time. This is because, as our emotions change, our personality may also shift to another set of characteristics momentarily. For example, the Energetic personality, when angry, may momentarily sound like an authoritative Driver. The Amiable, when in deep thought, may momentarily sound like an Analytic. Therefore, understanding vocal styles can not only give us insight as to a person's personality, but also their driving emotion under irregular conditions.

## Cold-Calling Scripts

Most people are afraid of the word "script". I was once... I thought that a script meant that I had to read something out loud word for word (referred to as "verbatim"). But not all scripts are meant to be, nor need to be, read verbatim (with the exception of some legal disclosures). A script is really just a pre-planned response to some situation or activity. I wake up every morning, get out of bed, have a shower, get dressed, and go out for coffee... and I do this every morning... my mornings are scripted. I don't always do it <u>exactly</u> the same... but the general idea is there... it's still a scripted morning.

Life is scripted! When you plant a tree... if certain conditions exist - the soil is good, the ground watered, etc. - the tree grows... If those conditions don't exist, then the tree dies. It has happened the same way for thousands of years, and it will continue to happen this way for thousands more. Almost everything is pre-planned. Kinda gets you thinking about the universe doesn't it?

My focus here will be on cold-call scripts, but consider other areas that could be scripted. Scripts allow you to react to situations, such as when prospects ask you questions, without feeling pressured, stressed or uncomfortable. Your brain doesn't have to search for an answer because you've already pre-programmed it. Just like our conversation about systems in chapter 1. So again, you always have to follow a script exactly the same every time... I would personally suggest that you don't, but a general plan or guideline, should be in effect.

Cold-calling, by the way, refers to calling someone whom you have not yet met (referred to as your cold market), as opposed to someone whom you already know, or whom you have been (formally or informally) introduced to through someone you already know (referred to as your warm market).

Cold-calling scripts should all include some basic parts, these are: ***1. Introduction:*** Tell the prospect who are, what company you work with, and why you are calling them (provide a reason for them to be attentive to your message, and gain their interest). ***2. Qualify and Engage:*** Discover if they have the right qualifications, and if it would make sense to continue with the call. ***3. Persuasion Statement:*** Give them a reason to be interested in the conversation, and draw them in. Features and benefits may also be included here. ***4. Call To Action:*** Get them to act! Whether that be to make a purchase, visit your website, accept additional information, or whatever you want them to do. Trial closes are considered a call-to-action.

Let's use the above ingredients in an example... If I was calling businesses to prospect for a new type of office software, my script may go something like this:

1. Good day John, my name is Dan, I'm calling from XYZ company... We're introducing our new office software that helps business owners like you get more done in less time... *[Introduction]*.

2. Would you be open to changing your office software if it meant cutting the amount of time you spend in front of your computer in half *[Qualifying question]*? (assume they say "yes")

3. Our new office software comes with its own voice-to-text component that is more advanced than anything you'll find in the market *[Persuasive - Comparative statement]*. This voice-to text component allows you to program your voice so you can speak directly to the software and it will type out whatever you speak as fast as you can speak *[Feature statement]*, saving you the time and effort of typing out your documents *[Benefit statement]*. It's is currently being used by some of the fastest growing companies in North America *[Persuasive - Association statement]*; and is quickly being accepted across the country *[Persuasive - Consensus statement]*.

4. I'm sure you'll really appreciate the way this software works, and would like a moment to stop by and show it to you. I have time available today at 2pm or tomorrow morning at 10am... Which of these would best suit your schedule *[Call-to-action - Alternative choice close]*?

You can see how each of the four parts mentioned earlier can come into play. Of course, our example script above could still be considered a little vague, and the software mentioned was purely for example purposes and does not actually exist at this time. You may also have more than one qualifying question.

An effective script will have potential responses for each possible answer that a prospect can provide. This means - Every time you ask a question in the script your prospect may respond in more than one way, and it only makes sense to have responses prepared for each possible answer the prospect may give... In part two of the mock script above, you noticed we asked "Would you be open to changing your office software if it meant cutting the amount of time you spend in front of your computer in half?" Here, the prospect may say "yes", or the prospect may say "no". You need to be prepared for each of these possible answers - Regardless of which answer the prospect gives, your response should lead back into the script, and aim to move the customer toward the call-to-action, or trial close.

Rather than designing one full cold-call script, design a series of small (paragraph-sized) scripts that can be used together in any order. Write the script down in full so that it's planned out as well as possible, but only memorize the key points of each mini-script.

**Voicemail Messages**

Voicemail messages should be treated as a form of short audio advertising. Pre-plan your voicemail message with a focus on the benefits that your product or services provides. The best voicemail messages will first gain the person attention and interest, and then provide a call to action, usually to direct the prospect to another piece of marketing or sales aid. Keep your voicemail short, enthusiastic and to the point.

Within 1-2 seconds of listening to the beginning of a voicemail message, people begin to pick up on certain cues that suggest what the remainder of the voicemail will be about. Most people will immediately delete voicemails that sound like a sales pitch, unless that message is capable of gaining their attention and interest within that first two seconds. Messages that are irrelevant to the prospect's needs goals and/or desires are also sure to get deleted quickly.

Do not use specifics in a voicemail message. Remember that the voicemail message should never attempt to do your selling for you, but rather only get them to follow through with your call to action. Instead, use generalizations that are more likely to appeal to a wider range of prospects, giving you a chance to qualify these prospects personally.

You may also consider creating an urgent sense of curiosity in order to compel the prospect to return your call. One way of doing this is to cut your message short, only providing a part of the message, and advise the prospect (within the message) to contact you (or otherwise visit your website) for the remainder of the message (i.e. These new widgets can do the job for half the price... Find out how much... visit www.Mywidgets.com).

## Sales Literature

Sales letters are no different from any other form of advertising. Maybe just a little longer... With this in mind, review all of the information on advertising in the previous chapter. Effective sales letters are designed using the A.I.D.A. formula: The first step is to get the reader's <u>attention</u>; then create a sincere <u>interest</u> in them regarding your offer; follow this by developing an insatiable <u>desire</u> to act; and finally, ask them to <u>act</u>. This formula, by the way, can be used in every aspect of your selling process... your sales speech, your sales letters, your presentations, etc.

The first step in getting their attention is to craft an interesting headline. Effective headlines generate enough interest and curiosity to make the reader want to go on and read the first paragraph. A few common ways to ensure the headline is interesting is to involve controversy, introduce something shocking, or appeal to something of deep interest to your target reader through the use of a bold statement or question such as...

"3 Guaranteed Methods of Making Money Fast!"

The above headlines would probably appeal to most people... At least long enough to get them to read the first few lines of an article...

Regardless of the headline that you use... The first paragraph of your sales letter should begin by grabbing the reader's attention again. This is very important as people treat written material as they would any advertising, so if you don't get their attention and interest in the first paragraph, they may never read the remainder of your letter. Statistically, the first three to six lines is all you have.

One of the best methods of gaining the reader's attention in the first paragraph is to appeal to the reader in some way. "Appeal" means that you begin with something in which the reader has a pre-determined interest (this makes target marketing very important). If they're already interested in the topic of conversation, they're likely to keep reading. Appeal to the reader's anxiety, fear, anger, passion, frustration or desire. You could also consider telling a short story within your letter, and then relating that story to your offer in some way; or educating the reader on a topic that would be of interest. If you were writing an automobile sales letter for instance, you may write something like this:

*"Last year, almost 13000 Canadian drivers traded in their used automobile for a new car... Now, they're all kicking themselves in the "you know what". If you were one of those lucky folks who thought about trading your car in last year - but didn't, pay special attention to the few lines below, and I will share with you a little secret that may change your life..."*

The above introduction would be attractive to someone who was interested in buying a new car. Wouldn't you want to know why you're lucky? Wouldn't you want to know what that secret is? You may then mention special deals that are available, special financing that is available, special buy-back programs that re-purchase their old car as a trade-in option, etc.

Interest can also be gained by appealing to their goals, desires or an area of personal gain. If you target market effectively, then you should already know what interests your target. Target groups will most often share similar interests. For instance, most medium-sized companies are seeking growth – Which means that if you can show them how to grow their business you can gain their interest. Most young working women are interested in special sale events at shopping centers. Will such assumptions work all the time…? No! But the general consensus says…! The more specific you are in narrowing your target groups, the better you can appeal to the specific interests of those groups and the people within them. Remember, that interest is generally gained through the self-interest principle, which essentially states that people are interested in themselves first. What's in it for them? How do they benefit?

Once you have the reader's interest, you have to keep it long enough to get your point across. Just because you have gained their interest (on some level) doesn't always mean they will act on that interest! The perfect sales letter will be able to convert the reader's interest, into an insatiable desire to move forward in some way; whether that be to make a phone call, send an email, or go to another form of marketing (i.e. a blog or a website, or a specific location, etc.). Desire is the key. It is an emotional… let me repeat that - An emotional response that propels the reader to <u>want</u> to move forward in some way. Fear, love, hate, greed, pain, desire… All emotions are very powerful in human motivation. Tell people how they can get exclusive offers, great deals, unique products, save time and money, benefit in some important way or get a product or result that they really want… What do you're prospects want???

Finally, as previously mentioned… The perfect sales letter will always include a call-to-action. This could be anything form "Call me" to "Email me" to "check out our website / blog". I personally like to write interesting call to actions such as "If you're curious enough to find out what this product can do for you, call (647) 700-0220".

# Concept #6
# Present Like A Master

*D*on't always expect that everybody in your audience will be listening to your presentation. It is more likely, that at any point in your presentation, you will find three types of people... Those who <u>are</u> listening, those who are slowly getting bored or losing interest, and those who are not listening at all. Watch for subtle cues and body-language that suggests you may need to change the pace a little.

If you find that more people are not listening, or many people (often) lose interest, you may want to consider changing your presentation... And you may need to do it on the fly (without notice). So what makes an effective presentation anyway?

The human brain tends to filter out everything that seems normal or ordinary. You can force yourself to pay attention to something for so long before you start drifting off... For most of us, that's about 20 minutes. It's when things are out of the ordinary that we tend pay greater attention... Greater attention = more memorability (the more we pay attention to things, the more memorable they become). People also tend to pay more attention to things that evoke emotional responses, and even more so when those responses are at a peak – This means that if you can get people to become afraid, angry, sad, happy, hopeful, etc., they will pay more attention to your presentation and content, and that content will have a greater effect on them.

Emotion... This is a key... That means you can NOT stand in front of the crowd and be un-moving, or monotonous. You need fluctuations in your voice and actions to appear interesting. As you keep reading, you'll find more information that will aid you in activating memory and providing effective presentations…

## Take Time To Prepare

For most of us, it makes sense to pre-plan our presentations. Of course, the majority of this book suggests that careful planning is always recommended. Aside from planning, you want to act out your plan in the most interesting way possible. The more interested your audience is, the more attentive they will be, and the more they will learn and retain the information within your presentation. That means you want to rehearse your plan before it's time to present. Rehearsing also helps automate your actions, at least to some degree, which aids in reducing stage fright or performance anxiety. A small word of caution though, regarding keeping the audience's interest… Take some care that your methods used to keep the audience's interest do not over-power the audience's ability to absorb the important information within your presentation - keep them focused on the information you want them to absorb, and not on you.

If your presentation is one that you will be presenting many times (which is true for most salespeople), review your presentation each time you perform and perfect it with each presentation. The Perfect Sales Pro knows that perfection does not happen immediately, it takes work and effort. Consider sitting down with a pen and paper shortly after you have given the presentation (and have left your audience), and writing down all the things that went right, and all the things that went wrong – And give yourself suggestions for improvement. Eventually (hopefully sooner than later), you'll have the perfect presentation. Keep reading, as there are other tools in this book to assist you in perfecting your presentation skills...

## Have A Hook!

Start your presentation with a "hook". A hook is an exciting introduction that grabs the audience's attention at the beginning of your presentation. Some successful ways to develop a hook may include: 1. Shock or Surprise 2. Direct questions 3. Ask a rhetorical question and answer it immediately. 4. Tell a short story 5. Dramatize a problem 6. Recite a quote 7. Introduce a particular scenario.

## Memory

The goal of any presentation is to get people to walk away and remember the key points of the presentation. Really good presenters can get the audience to remember the entire content of the presentation. Great presenters can get them to remember not only the content of the presentation, but the presentation itself. The perfect presenter, can get them not only to remember, but to yearn for more.

If you want your audience to remember your presentation, then it's important to understand how memory works. While this book will not give you a complete disclosure of the inner-workings of the mind, we will discuss four of the most important principles to keep in mind when planning your presentation:

## Primacy / Recency

Studies have shown that when presented with information, lists or stories, people are more likely to remember what they hear or read first, and what they hear or see last. This is called the primacy - recency effect. With this in mind, when you plan your presentation, try to plan the most important things that you want to say at the beginning and at the end of your presentation. You can often re-engage the effect by re-organizing a presentation so that it appears more like several short presentations. TherIf you have important information to present during the middle of your presentation, make sure that you re-engage the audience's attention and regain their level of interest before proceeding.

> One way to re-engage the audience's interest is to pause the presentation briefly for a question and answer period. Either the audience can ask you questions, or you can ask the audience questions. A short period involving 4-5 questions will allow the primacy-recency effect to be re-engaged when you continue the presentation. You may also consider a break for a short story, audience-involved exercises, tell a joke or two, or provide a brief review/summary.

> Studies have shown that audiences listening to a continuous flow of information begin to lose interest after about 20 minutes… Personally, I like to include some form of short break every 10 minutes! Give a story, tell a joke, play a game, or find some interesting way to allow the audience to relax a bit.

## Repetition

Memory is engraved through repetition. Few people will ever remember what you tell them after the first time. There are, of course, some exceptions to this, but in general, people need to hear things several times before it becomes a part of their long-term memory. One way to arrange a memorable presentation is to use the following three-step formula: ***1. Tell them what you're going to tell them  2. Tell them  3. Then tell them what you've told them.*** In simple terms, prepare the audience for what is about to come by providing them an overview, give your presentation, and then summarize or recap the key points of that presentation.

You may also want to choose key points during the presentation and repeat those key points. If you do this, keep it interesting by changing the tonality and inflection of your voice, perhaps excite some emotion by adding the appropriate emphasis.

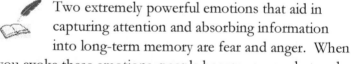 Two extremely powerful emotions that aid in capturing attention and absorbing information into long-term memory are fear and anger. When you evoke these emotions, people become more alert and this allows for a greater degree of information to be converted into long-term memory.

## Heightened Interest

Our ability to retain information is skyrocketed when we first tell ourselves that what we are about to learn is important to us… but a general interest in the information is not enough. The effect occurs when we are emotionally excited about what we are learning at the time of learning it. Even more so, when we can imagine ourselves utilizing the information within the very near future.

 Help you audience understand the importance of the information that you are presenting, and peak their interest, by letting them know how they can use that information in the near future. Use verbs, adjectives, and adverbs that help the audience create vivid imagery in their mind of themselves performing those actions. Consider doing the same for your final call to action!

**The RAS**

Located at the top of the stem of the brain, the Reticular Activating System (RAS) is one of the brain's filters that helps us determine what is important, and what is not. It controls the level to which we are alert, attentive and responsive to incoming information. It also causes us to ignore or downplay information (sensory activity) which is deemed less important. When the brain (particularly the RAS) decides that something is important, it becomes more memorable. Here's a special note on how you can use the RAS…

You can program the mind to pay attention to particular details by telling yourself that they are important, this programming process is called "installing a reticular activator"… When I use to drive a Ford, I never took the time to notice how many other types of cars were occupying the roads in my city… The moment I bought my first BMW, I began noticing how many other BMWs were on the roads in my area. That's not because there was a sudden influx of BMW drivers; its because I simply never noticed them before! Whether consciously or unconsciously, at some point I had told myself to pay attention to BMW's – And I did! Maybe you've had a similar experience.

When you give yourself such a command, you program yourself according to the heightened interest principle (described above). This command is then transferred to your RAS which allows the relevant information to be accessed by your consciousness. But what if someone else gives the command? What then? Well… The funny thing happens when someone else gives you a command that is perceived as being important, or of significant value… You actually repeat the command to yourself (in your head) in order to allow it to be processed by your mind. As you process the command, you are, in fact, installing a reticular activator.

> Install a reticular activator in your audience's mind by telling them what to do in a particular circumstance.

As they repeat the command back to themselves, they will effectively be programming their unconscious to perform that particular action when the circumstance arrives. If you were selling vacation packages to Hawaii, for example, you could say "The next time you drive home from work, think about how nice it would be to go on vacation in Hawaii". You may even follow this by with a short description of an experience they may have (to make the command more vivid), such as "lying on the beach, being served by hula-girls, the wind rushing through your hair". Want to amplify this effect, simply ask them how they would feel under those circumstances. With this reticular activator, if enough interest was gained prior to the command, your prospect would be most likely to think about Hawaii on their next drive home from work.

## Flow Structure

From beginning to end, there will be a series of stages through which your presentation will flow. Recognize these stages, and design your presentation accordingly. Here are a few ideas: ***1. Chronological Flow:*** Give the presentation in terms of time - begin with the earliest time and move to the present or future. ***2. Problems and Solution:*** Present a series of problems, and disclose how those problems can / will be solved. ***3. Features and Benefits:*** Present the features of your offer, and the benefits the offer can provide.

Consider how your presentation will transition from one phase to another. Will the transition occur logically in some given order? Will it transition by flowing from one related concept to another concept? Or will you have some repeated theme that occurs through each transition stage?

Prepare your presentation in advance. Most well designed presentation will have 3-4 phases, which means 3-4 transitions. Consider adding dramatic appeal by changing the emotion used in each phase. For instance, you may begin your presentation attempting to capture the heart(s) of your audience (empathetic), and transition to a logical phase where you provide statistics, and then a strong emotional phase again where generate anger to a peak, and you may demand action!

## Games

There are two things that people will always be interested in... Games and stories. From childhood days, most of us learn to enjoy games and stories, and this enjoyment becomes embedded into our identity.

There a variety of verbal games that you can play with prospects to get them involved in the presentation. Sometimes, you don't even need them to be directly involved, but simply to get them to imagine the responses to themselves. One word of caution though, games - even verbal games - require correct timing. Don't assume that everybody wants to play games all of the time.

Some verbal games that you can play with prospects include: Guess The Answer; Two Truths And A Lie; Would You Rather; and Fill In The Blank games.

## Stories

Stories are especially powerful and persuasive tools to get prospects emotionally engaged in your conversation. Stories can put the listener into an almost trance-like state, open their minds, paint mental imagery, and get them to conceive the unconceivable. With that much power, it almost makes sense to become a master of story-telling.

I suggest having your story pre-planned. When you have pre-planned your story, you avoid fumbling with your words or having to search for the next thing to say. When presenting, you don't necessarily need to recite your story word for word, but at least have a basic sequence of concepts.

**Story Plot**

The first step to good story-telling is to consider what your plot will be about. The plot is the main idea behind the story itself... What will the story REALLY be about? If you were to day "This story is about..." how would you finish that sentence? Will it be about revenge? Or may it be about change or transformation, or maybe about personal experience. It may be about solving a riddle or a mystery. Maybe... It will have two or three plots combined into one story!

## Story Type

The next step is to consider what type of story it will be. There are essentially six types of stories: Myths; sagas; fables; parables; folk-tales; and fairy-tales. Your story may also be fiction, true-life events; or possibly a little bit of both.

## Story (Transportation) Techniques

Stories don't always have to begin from beginning to end. The story-telling world (including the movie industry) has created a series of techniques to make stories more interesting, by shifting parts of a story around, stepping outside of the norm of a story or including stories within stories. For example, a technique called Chekov's Gun allows for the introduction of an object at the beginning of the story, which is left rather unclear as to why it has been introduced - until the end of the story, where it becomes a major part of the unraveling. There are many such techniques that can be useful in pre-planning your story. Most of these can be readily found in my next book: *The Master Sales Manual*.

# Sales Presentations

Sales presentation take a little additional care. Utilize all of the presentation techniques above, but consider a few additional pieces of knowledge and techniques as outlined here.

## Three Stages of Readiness

The first thing to consider in a sales presentation, is to determine how ready your audience is for a solution. There are essentially three stages of readiness: ***1. The Knowing Customer:*** Also referred to as the contemplation stage. These prospects know that a problem exists, but are not ready to deal with it. ***2. The Solution Seeker:*** This is also referred to as the ready stage. These prospects know that a problem exists, and are seeking a solution. ***3. The Clueless Customer:*** This is called the pre-contemplation stage. These prospects don't know the problem exists. You may need to make them aware of the problem!

The Perfect Sales Pro knows that the type of audience that you are presenting to effects the details and delivery of the presentation. To the clueless customer, present the problem first. To the knowing customer, present the need to act. Finally, to the solution seeker, present the benefits of your solution over the alternatives. With this in mind, it is important to have a good understanding of who your audience is, and what stage they are at. Find out as much as you can about your audience prior to the presentation, and use this insight to design the presentation itself.

## Features & Benefits

As part of the presentation process, a list of important features and benefits should be reviewed. A feature is a distinctive attribute or aspect of your product that is of some importance or significance. A benefit, is an explanation of why a particular feature is important, and how it will help the prospect in some way, shape or form.

Let's say you were trying to sell a new computer with twice the processing speed. You could say "This computer has a very fast processor, twice as fast as anything else on the market (feature), which will allow you to run multiple programs, multi-task and get your work done faster (benefit). If you were a realtor selling a three bedroom house to a two-person family, you could say "Sure the house has three bedrooms (feature) which leaves you a nice-size area for that home-office to do all of your work (benefit)"

Prospects don't always associate product features and benefits automatically. Some prospects even attempt to find a reason not to buy when presented with an unattended feature. Don't leave your features unattended, provide your prospect with a benefit associated to each feature. You may even provide them with two or three benefits for each feature. Try to find benefits that are directly related to their needs or desires, but even if the benefits you provide are not directly appropriate, it gets them thinking for reasons to buy instead of reasons not to.

## USP

If you're presenting to prospects who have never had the opportunity to review products such as yours, review all of the features and benefits of your product. Sometimes, however, prospects have been "shopping around", or have a previous understanding of similar products, and it is not necessary to review each and every feature of the product. While your product may have several important features and benefits, you should focus heavily on those that provide some differentiation. Differentiation refers to those features and benefits that set your product aside from similar competitive products. If you could choose just one single differentiation that would be more important than anything else – This would be your USP or Unique Selling Proposition.

 Focus most heavily on your Unique Selling Proposition.

## Emotional Benefits

As mentioned in chapter 2 under the Buying Cycle, people make their buying decisions emotionally. With this in mind, when you present your offer, make sure you review the emotional benefits that your product will bring. The main emotional benefit to the prospect is known as the ESP – Emotional Selling Proposition.

Studies have shown that most of our brain's logical functions come from the left side of the brain; whilst most of its creative and emotional functions come from the right side of the brain. In most people, the two sides of the brain do not work well simultaneously, meaning that the more we attempt to process logic, the less creative and emotional we become; but more importantly, the more we process creativity and emotion, the less logical we become.

 This all means that the more you raise your prospect's emotions regarding your offer, the less he will attempt to analyze and scrutinize it. Bring your prospect(s) to an emotional peak in regards to your offer... Focus heavily on your "Emotional Selling Proposition" (ESP).

Emotional selling propositions are used by most major brands, and they understand the power of this so well that, sometimes, they exaggerate in the disclosure of their USP in their marketing and advertising. Volvo, for instance, has a reputation of being a "safe" car. If you want to buy a car for your wife and kids, buy a Volvo. There is no scientific or mechanical data that concludes how a Volvo is safer than many other available cars on the market, but through repeated use of their emotional selling proposition they have developed a reputation, an image, and a brand... Being recognized as "safe" gives Volvo's target market the feeling that they seek – A comfortable reassurance that they are in good hands. But not all drivers are seeking a "safe" car. Not all drivers value safety over everything else (though maybe they should). Some drivers primarily focus on comfort, while others seek power, while others still seek simply to look "cool" or to fit in with their community or peers or focus groups. ESP's catch their attention and drive their interest… What's yours?

# A.I.D.A

The AIDA formula was briefly described in Chapter 5 in our section on Sales Letters. It is such a useful formula for any form of marketing, advertising or presentation. When engaged in a sales presentation, it is especially important to make use of this formula - Let's look at an example:

Imagine for a moment, that you've spent some preparing for a major presentation at your clients home. You get there and knock on the door, and they invite you in, and suggest that the presentation could be held in the living room. You all sit down, have coffee, and then you begin to get into your presentation... You're about to get into the important aspects of your offer, and your client's children come home from school... they're a bit noisy. One of the children come to sit in the living room and turns on the television. The other goes outside to unleash the dog... and the dog runs straight into the house. The house becomes a bit noisy and distractive... But you're a trooper, so you continue on with the presentation, you do your best to get the benefits across and create a desire to buy... And at the end of your presentation you get the same response you always do: "We'll have to think about it!"

The problem here is not that you're offer was not enticing... The problem is that your offer was not REALLY understood. You didn't have their full attention. You lost their unwavering devotion to your presentation.

Let's look at this again... Some salespeople believe that, if there are no distractions, you must have the audience's attention. There is a slight complication in this belief... I've given presentations to large and small groups of people... and I've learned that it's up to me to keep the audience engaged. The average attention span of any individual in a presentation is about 20 minutes. After that, if they are not fully interested, or otherwise engaged in the presentation, they begin to seek other things to occupy their minds - leading to a lack of attention. Some studies show that people want to feel emotionally involved every 5-6 minutes. The type of audience, the setting, and the presentation may all play a different part in this... Certainly a presentation in large groups will differ from a presentation in somebody's home or in a retail store. In a cold-call over the telephone for instance, you must gain their interest within 2-3 minutes.

The more interested your audience is in your presentation, the more likely they will gain a desire for the offer... Without interest, they definitely will have no desire for you product. Desire is described as an insatiable "want". The interesting thing is that when people "want" something strongly enough, it quickly becomes a "need" in their own mind. By this, I mean that people will trick themselves into believing that they absolutely need to have something, if their desire for it is strong enough.

Even better than desire, is recurring desire. When people want something, and their desire for it is activated over and over again, the desire grows stronger each time it is activated. So if your presentation is of any significant length, choose one or two important benefits and revisit those benefits several times throughout your presentation.

 Throughout your presentation, revisit their desires often, through questions and information. Don't leave it up to your prospects to create a link between their desires and your information.

Finally, you must ask, (or direct) people to act. Tell them how they can take advantage of all the benefits you've spoken about throughout your presentation. Give them a reason to act now! Make it easy for them to do so.

## Stage Fright

Probably the hardest thing about giving presentations, is dealing with your own emotions. People can become so emotional before or during a presentation, that they begin to imagine things that haven't yet happened, aren't happening or may never happen. It's the idea of it happening, that is the main cause of stage fright. This causes mental and physical apprehension, which then turns into anxiety (which may occur on different levels). Most people think of anxiety as a psychological response, and it is - however, during an anxiety response, a rush of adrenaline is released into the bloodstream affecting the nervous system, which then afflicts our motor skills (our ability to control our body).

Some ways to deal with stage fright include repetition or rehearsal of your presentation; use of breathing and relaxation techniques; and increasing physical activity to put your body and nervous system at par.

You can learn more about presentation skills in The Master Sales Manual, and subsequent books.

# Concept #7

## Sell Like A Pro

*B*eyond the presentation, selling involves three basic skills... Asking good questions, handling objections, and closing the deal. In this chapter, we will discuss some effective ways to do these. For more information on each of these crucial topics, please refer to *The Master Sales Manual*.

## Questions

When you ask someone a question, it grabs their attention, and pulls their concentration in toward you as they attempt to answer the question. Questions allow you to discover their needs and desires, control the conversation in the direction you want, isolate interests and concerns, and arouse emotions in the prospect (as they consider the answers to your questions).

The Perfect Sales Pro will ask a lot of questions during a conversation with a prospect. I've always said myself "If you let people talk long enough, they will disclose their entire world to you". I often get through lengthy conversations without talking more than 10% of the time. When they do most of the talking, the conversation usually ends with the other person thinking "Wow, that was a wonderful conversation... I really like that guy"... Of course it was a wonderful conversation - They did all the talking!

A word of warning though... Be careful what type of questions you ask – Personality, relationship, time and circumstance (context) can all effect how people will react to certain questions. Even the right questions at the wrong moment can arouse negative feelings. Consider using softening questions and statements to pre-empt the question you want to ask – Softening questions include "Do you mind if I ask…"; "Would you mind settling my curiosity about…"; "Would you be offended if I ask…" etc. You can also use softening statements such as "I'm just curious…"; "This question is quite important…"; "Before moving forward, I need to know…" etc. Pre-empting a question with softeners such as these portrays an extra degree of respect, and when you approach people with respect, they will be more than likely to respond in kind.

The softeners above work well because you are giving the prospect some reason why you are asking the particular question. People also tend to become offended or irritated or even find it intrusive, if you ask too many questions. If you must ask many or multiple questions, give people a reason for the series of questions first, and they will be more at ease for the questioning process. An example would be: "Would you mind if I asked a few questions to confirm how I may be able to best assist you?"

People will usually enjoy talking about two things - Themselves… and those things they have an interest in. This is called the self-interest principle. The more you gear your conversation, your questions and your statements to them and their interests, the more involved they will be in the conversation, and the more they will appreciate the conversation.

When you get people talking about themselves and/or their interests, lead the conversation in the direction you want (through effective questions and statements), and encourage the prospect to tell you more, which can be done simply by showing interest in what they are saying.

## Open & Close Ended Questions

There are some basic considerations in deciding what type of question to ask, most notably, you want to decide if your question is open-ended or close-ended. A close-ended question is one that requires the prospect to choose between the answers that you provide... The most common close-ended questions require a "yes" or "no" answer, however, you may ask a question that requires a choice of any answers you wish. With close-ended questions, you shouldn't provide more than two or three choices from which the prospect may choose, as any more than this can get confusing (which is called the "smorgasbord effect"), and the prospect may choose to avoid the question all together.

Close-ended questions allow for specifics to be answered, and aid in directing the conversation. Open-ended questions allow the prospect to answer in any manner at all. They allow for the greatest degree of conversational development and aid in building the relationship. If you want to discover more information and get the prospect talking, ask open-ended questions, listen attentively, and show sincere interest in what the prospect is saying (provide minor feedback such as hmmm, ahhh, ohhh, really?, etc.) - And the prospect is likely to keep talking... Perhaps forever (ok... maybe not forever!).

Use close-ended questions when you want to direct the conversation and lead the prospect toward a particular answer. Use open-ended questions when you want the prospect to provide you more information about his situation or thought-pattern. When using open-ended questions, the Perfect Sales Pro will listen closely - Not only to what the prospect is saying, but also to the meaning the prospect is putting forward.

**Leading & Funnel Questions**

Once you have allowed for some development in the relationship, you want to start driving the prospect's answers toward your product in a positive manner. This is often referred to in the sales industry as "Leading a horse to water". The goal is to allow the prospect to think he is deciding to make a buying decision all on his own. Two methods of doing this are by asking Leading questions and Funnel Questions. Leading questions are effective because they directly suggest to the prospect how the question should be answered. An example of a leading question would be "Aren't you learning a lot from this little book?"... This is quite different from asking "Are you learning something from this little book?"

Funnel questioning is a technique in which a short series of questions are asked that either require the prospect to answer in broad terms, and move toward specifics, or vice versa (if the funnel is upside down!). A three step example of this would be "**1.** Would you like to learn about sales? **2.** Would you like to learn general or specific information about sales? **3.** What specifically would you like to learn about sales?" *(Whatever your answer, you're certain to find it in my next book - The Master Sales Manual).*

**Tag Questions**

Tag questions are also very important in sales, as they allow you to make a direct statement, and (almost) force the answer that you want them to give. Tag questions are little (usually two word) questions added to the end of a statement that convert a statement into a question. There are positive and negative tag questions. Positive tag questions are generally used with a negative statement, and include: Is it?; Could it?; Would it?; Should it?; Can it?; Does it?; and Will it? Negative tag questions, on the other hand, are generally used with a positive statement, and include: Isn't it?; Couldn't It? Wouldn't It?; Shouldn't It?; Can't It?; Doesn't it?; Won't it?

An example of good use of tag questions would be… "You do want the benefits that this product can provide, <u>don't you?</u>" Let's assume that you're selling insurance to a family with two children… You could say "You do want the peace of mind that a good insurance policy like this one can provide, don't you?" (Of course this assumes that you have already described the insurance program prior to asking this question). This example uses a negative tag question (don't you?).

Tag questions can also be used to lead the conversation in the direction that you want. You can use tag questions to get the prospect to agree with you, thus moving the conversation toward the purchase of your product.

In the following example, the first three questions are tag questions designed to get the prospect to sell himself on buying a new Corvette after a test drive (the fourth question is a closing question): **1.** "Everything else seems to go just right when you feel like a superstar, doesn't it?" **2.** "You do want to feel like a superstar don't you?" **3.** "… And tell me, when you drive through the streets with this brand new Corvette, you do feel like a superstar don't you?" **4.** Can you find any reason, then, that you should deny yourself that feeling?

**Alternative Choice Questions**

Another very popular type of question is the Alternative Choice question. The idea behind this, is that you never want to ask your prospect if he wants your product... Rather, you ask the prospect if he wants it "this way" or "that way". Either way he answers, he has suggested that he <u>wants</u> your product, and this allows you to move toward closing the sale. An example of an alternative choice question is: "Would you like this in red or in blue?" In the previous example, whether they choose the red or the blue, they have also chosen to purchase the item.

# Objections

Handling objections is one key area that many salespeople find difficult. Probably because in order to handle an objection, there is some degree of confrontation involved. When a prospect says "No thank you", it's easy to simply say "That's ok" and move on. It's much harder to say "now hold on, you're just not thinking this through clearly!" Of course I wouldn't suggest using those exact words... but that is the general frame of mind.

**Objections vs. Excuses**

Your time as a salesperson is important... You have much to do in order to be effective and successful. The Perfect Sales Pro will learn to judge prospects very quickly and decide whether the prospect has valid objections or not. Be caution, then, as to where you spend your time. Many objections are really not objections at all. An objection carries the mentality "I would... but..." Often, the prospect has already made up his mind not to make the purchase at all, and no matter what you say, you're not going to get him to buy. These prospects will often give you excuses that sound like objections. They may be attempting to be kind, or at least not to be so blunt, yet it is important to learn to recognize the difference between objections and excuses. This will come with experience. Classify these prospects and possibly reconsider if they were really good prospects at all... If you truly believe they are potential prospects, then classify them accordingly as discussed under chapter 4.

**Three Types of Objections**

There are essentially three types of objections, they are:
***1. Situational:*** These occur because of some type of situation. Overcoming these objections requires some problem solving skills to aid the prospect in overcoming the specific situation. ***2. Conditional:*** These occur because of some perceived condition. Overcoming these is usually a matter of aiding the prospect to find a solution, or otherwise by changing the prospects psychology.
***3. Informational:*** These occur because the prospect does not have all the information needed to make the decision. To overcome these, provide the prospect with more information as needed, and consider ways to amplify the value in your offer.

Let's just look at a few examples to ensure it all makes sense... A situational objection could be "I don't have enough money". This is a situation which could easily be solved with a loan or a payment plan.

An example of a conditional objection could be "I have to ask my wife". This is conditional because if the wife says ok, the prospect will likely go ahead with the purchase (assuming that asking the wife wasn't just an excuse). You could either get the wife on the phone and get her ok (problem solving) or change the prospect's psychology by getting him to agree that he could make the decision without his wife. An informational objection could be "I'm not interested in this car because it doesn't have an MP3 player". You could advise the prospect that an MP3 player is one of the bells and whistles that you can offer extra. You may even offer to give him a great deal on it if he buys now! Most prospects will simply say "I'm not interested", and it is your responsibility as a salesperson to employ specificity as discussed in chapter 3.

**The First Objection**

Ninety-nine percent of prospects will say no to you when you first approach them. You can get around this by getting them to approach you... That, however, requires great marketing skills *(possibly covered in a later book)*. The real problem is that, although people love to buy, people are afraid to be sold. They are afraid of being coerced into doing something they may not truly want to do, or may later regret doing – Even if they really 'want' to do it anyway. They want to make their own decision, at their own pace, in their own way. In short, they really don't like salespeople.

Many companies and retail chains have forgone the term "salesperson" or "sales associate", and prefer to name their salespeople more inviting names such as "customer service associate" or even "customer advocate". This rebranding aids in creating a different frame of mind in reference to the salesperson... at least until they begin to sell.

Back to objections... The very first objection that a prospect will give you is usually an instinctive response designed to repel you as a salesperson. Most of the time, the prospect hasn't really thought about the answer, and may even later regret having given the objection. It's simply an automatic reaction (They may just as well hold up a crucifix and some garlic and shout "away – demon... away!").

My wife buys shoes every month... And she buys them every month from the same store... But every time she walks into the store to buy shoes, the sales associate asks "Can I help you" and her response is always the same: "No thanks, I'm just looking"... I'm sure you've never heard that before!!!

Most retail customers are exactly the same... But they don't just walk into a store to look, they walk in because something about the store or its products attract them. I can almost guarantee that your prospects are doing the same to you. Now... My wife, like most people, loves to shop, because it allows her to imagine herself owning all kinds of different things. And like most people, she loves to buy, because the feeling of owning something new is stimulating and exhilarating. But like most people, she hates to be sold to – because she wants to feel like to she is the one who decided to make the purchase; and she doesn't want feel like some salesperson tricked her into buying something she didn't want to buy, or had no business buying in the first place. Consciously or unconsciously, she thinks about these things, and formulates a response designed to cast the salesperson away "Nope… just looking… thanks!"

From time to time, that first objection that a prospect shouts out may actually be a valid one… This may happen if the prospect has previous experience with the product or similar products. In such a case… Use objection handling techniques as described below. Nine times out of ten, that first objection will simply be an instinctive response designed to get you to go away. Find a way to bypass these objections and continue the conversation. Depending on the context of the situation, you may choose to simply ignore the objection all together and continue the conversation, or offer to answer the objection at the end of your presentation (many times the presentation will answer the objection or the prospect may forget he asked). You may even have a mini-presentation designed just to get your 'foot in the door'.

**Minor Objections**

Minor objections are those that aren't directed at your product or offer, the most common of which is "I can't afford it". Minor objections often require a degree of problem solving skill. The prospect hasn't said "no" to your offer, but has given you some other non-specific reason why they can't or won't buy from you.

Minor objections are often caused by a lack of urgent desire. Often, if people want something bad enough, they will find the money to buy it. This, of course, may vary depending on the price-point of the product (i.e. some people really can't afford a new Corvette). Below, we'll discuss some ways to overcome this…

## Objection Handling Techniques

There are various methods commonly in practice to assist in handling objections. The problem with most objections is that they are not REALLY objections, as discussed earlier, they are broad generalizations of a concept designed to make the salesperson go away. In chapter 3 we discussed specificity - It is extremely difficult to handle a non-specific objection. Let's take a look at an example… Assume you are selling widgets to XYZ Company, and the CEO says "I'm not interested!" What do you do? Do you accept that as an answer? "I'm not interested" is not an objection, it is a broad generalization… You don't know why he's not interested, or what specifically about the offer he is not interested in. It would then be necessary for to ask questions such as "That's fine, but let me ask, what specifically about the offer is it that doesn't interest you?" You may even consider an attempt to force an answer from him by suggesting a few possible reasons "Would it be… The price, the color of my widgets, or possibly the size?" Even if it were neither of these suggestions that he wasn't interested in, he would more likely to give me a more precise response.

A short word of caution when using phrases such as "that's ok" or "that's fine"… If you allow a pause after the use of such phrases, you give the prospect a way out – He will surely interrupt and close the conversation. Make sure that you move swiftly into the next part of your sentence or questioning; or otherwise use an intermediate conjunction (such as "and", "but", "or", etc.) to let the prospect know you have more to say.

I also wouldn't suggest simply asking the prospect directly "Why aren't you interested?!!", or any similar direct question, as prospects tend to view this as abrupt, rude, and unprofessional – And generally tend to become very offended at such direct questions. A few effective ways to gain a specific objection from the prospect, is to use funnel questioning and objection chunking *(as described below)*.

## Funnel Questioning For Objections

With funnel questioning, you begin with a broad objection, and you ask questions that penetrate deeper into the precise reason for the objection until you have a satisfactory answer… One that you can handle effectively. An example of this would be "That's ok, but is it the item or the offer that you're not interested in?"; "What about the offer is it you're not interested in, the price, the agreement, or the terms?"; "Is the price per unit too high, or might it be the total cost that seems to be the issue?" Assuming he says it's the total cost, you can consider giving him discount for bulk purchase. If he had said it was the price per unit, you would need to dig deeper by asking "what type of budget are you working with?" (qualifying the prospect). Again, the more specific an answer you can get, the better you can arm yourself in handling that specific objection.

## Objection Chunking

Objection chunking is similar to funnel questioning, except that it does not have to occur in such as specific transition from generalization to specifics. You can break down the objection in any way that makes sense at the time. For instance "I understand that you're not interested... Would it be the price, the type of widget, or possibly the terms of the offer that you're not interested in?"

**Attitude Change**

Another common method of handling objections is to get prospect to become more open-minded about possibilities. You do this by using words such as "What if..."; "Consider..."; "Possible"; "Plausible"; "Options", etc. People often approach a situation with preset expectations and/or a preset attitude – If you can shift their attitude, you can begin to move things forward in a favorable direction. An example may be "What if it were possible to... Would you..." (What if it were possibly to lower your expenses on your purchase of widgets, and get far better value for your dollar, would you consider switching companies?". When using this method, appeal to their self-interest. There are many similar questions and question combinations using this type of wording that will provide great results.

Another method of changing the prospect's attitude is by providing new information that the prospect may not have been aware of. This is especially useful if the prospect's environment (legal, political, technological, etc) is changing. I once sold security alarms, and found that I was able to increase sales dramatically providing homeowners and business owners information about recent break-ins within their local area – The local environment had changed, and I was able to appeal to fear.

## Closing The Sale

There are many types of sales closes, probably more than I can count, and many of them have been known by multiple names... But there's really only one true close... And that happens when either the contract is signed, or a transaction has been performed - Preferably an exchange of money for a service or product. Everything else is preemptive. All other closes are actually trial-closes or minor closes - A close designed to move the prospect in the direction of the sale, and establish the likelihood of making the sale.

**Always Be Closing**

Use trial closes consistently throughout your presentation. They allow you to gauge the prospect and gain a good sense of how ready the prospect is to buy. Any basic sales training will teach you that you must use the ABC's of selling - Always Be Closing. Some will suggest there are three best times to use a trial close - Close Early, Close Often, and Close late.

**Establish Value**

Don't attempt to close until you first establish sufficient value for the prospect. Attempting to close the sale without first providing the prospect with sufficient value (reason to buy) will result in a loss of trust (the prospect will think you are just there to make a sale rather than to assist him in making a purchase). Remember, that in everything we do, people are always judging cost vs. value, and if there is no (or little) value, then the cost becomes greater. Make every closing process educational for the prospect... Tell them something new that you hadn't mentioned before, preferably something that would be of interest or value to them. Sometimes, the smallest piece of information or value could be enough to tip the sale in your favor.

 If you provide the prospect with information without knowing ahead of time where their interests lie, ask them if the information you've provided is of interest to them. If they say "yes", you have the opportunity to tell them more. If they say "no", you have the opportunity ask them what would be of interest to them. Do NOT just continue providing "irrelevant" information (see "relevancy" in chapter 2).

**Create Urgency**

Another important key is to establish urgency in your sale. Possibly give them an offer that is only available for a limited time. For example: If you travelled to a prospect's office, consider giving them a discount proportionate to the transportation cost and value of your time in returning to their office to complete a transaction *(Mr. prospect, it would cost me $X to come back here again, if you buy now, I'll give you a discount of $X)*. You could use almost any reason, but give them a reason to buy now instead of later!

**Keep It Simple**

Make it simple for your prospect to conclude the sale. Time and effort are valuable assets to your prospect. This means that the more of the prospects time or effort that is required to close the sale, the higher the cost of the purchase becomes in the mind of the prospect. A $100 purchase that only takes a few minutes and no effort is still considered a $100 purchase; but when that same purchase takes 30-40 minutes of their time, and requires them to "jump through hoops" so to speak, the purchase is considered far more costly. If the amount of time and effort is too great, regardless of the dollar value of the sale, the prospect may choose not to make the purchase at all.

Corporate purchases are quite different, in that it is generally acknowledged that these purchases require more time and a greater degree of effort, however, prospects of all types have a general idea as to how much time and effort they are willing to give for each type of purchase. Actually, by the time they are ready to buy, they have probably visualized themselves going through the steps of buying at least once (if not several times). The Perfect Sales Pro will offer to do much of the work for them. For example: If paperwork is involved, fill out all the paperwork and send them a copy that only requires a review (to ensure everything is correct) and a signature

## Closing Techniques

Here we describe a few commonly used closing techniques. Remember that these techniques only aid in moving the prospect closer to a real close – The signing of a contract or the completion of a transaction. Also keep in mind that there are many identified closing techniques, and these few by no means represent them all. I would lastly like to mention a short word of caution: There are many closing techniques designed to be shrewd, or even misleading – I do not promote any of these methods and suggest that you evaluate any such techniques prior to use. Lying to, or cheating, your prospects is a sure way to lose valuable relationships, repeat business and referrals.

Below is a small sample of closing techniques that I do promote:

### Alternative Choice Close

The Alternative Choice Close uses an alternative choice question to direct the prospect toward closing the sale. As mentioned earlier, you never want to give the prospect the choice as to whether or not he wants to buy the product, instead, you want to ask the prospect if he wants "this way" or "that way". For example: "Would you like to take it home with your today, or would you like me to package your purchase and ship it to you?"

## Comparison Close

The Comparison close is a simple close in which you compare your product to the competitive products or other alternatives your product. This is effective because, as people, we naturally think in terms of contrast (apples to oranges). It is usually only necessary to compare against the most popular competitive product, or possibly the two-three most popular products. The goal is to provide the prospect with a competitive differentiation that would be perceived as some value. For example: "We may not be the biggest, but we don't charge you for services you don't use either, as a result, we're are more economical".

When creating differentiation, keep in mind that there is more to a sale than finances. You may want to focus on service, quality, relationship, or anything else. A small company, for example, can compete with larger companies by focusing on how they build more personal relationships with their clients (everybody hates to be treated like "just another number").

## Sharp Angle Close

The Sharp Angle Close is a negotiate close that gives the perception that you are trying to meet them half way. This close uses language such as "If I could... Would you..." For example: "If I could give you free shipping, would you buy today?"

## Similar Situation Close

The Similar Situation close is one that takes advantage of "consensus", where you show how other people who are just like the prospect, have benefited from making the purchase. A popular example of this is the Feel Felt Found method, which uses the following formula: "I understand how you <u>feel</u>, some of my current customers have <u>felt</u> the same way, but what they <u>found</u> was was..."; You could also simply tell the prospect directly about others who have benefited (i.e. Your neighbor Mary owns one of these, and when I followed-up a week later she was still excited about owning it).

A Reverse Similar Situation close does just the opposite, it is designed to show the prospect how others who are just like him, have not made a purchase and now regret not doing so. An example would be "The last time this offer was available, my cousin John decided to go with another company, and he now pays twice as much for his service."

## Yes-Set Close

The yes-set close is a simple close which is designed to gain the prospect's agreement on a series of minor points, each of which leads to his agreement on the final purchase decision. The key here, is to ask questions to which you know the prospect is sure to answer affirmatively. A form of funnel questioning is often effective here. An example of this close would be "You are interested in new widgets aren't you?" (The prospect answers "yes"); "And you want to get the best value don't you?" (The prospect answers "Yes"); "And you are happy with the service that I've provided you today, aren't you?" (The prospect answers

"Yes"); so can you find any reason not to buy from me today?

# Concept #8

## Use Persuasive Communication

Once you have mastered the previous seven chapters, which should give you a great start to mastering sales, you can then begin using more advanced persuasive communication to help you in the selling process. Don't kid yourself though, there's still lots to learn on the previous seven concepts... We merely touched the top of the surface. You can either research these topics yourself, or find them in my next book: *The Master Sales Manual*.

In this chapter we take a look at influence, persuasion and negotiations. These are advanced level topics, of course we are not attempting, here, to provide an extremely deep investigation – We will, however, review the absolute necessities.

## Influence

Persuasion and influence go hand in hand. Whilst persuasion is the ability to get someone to act immediately, influence is the ability to create a longer lasting change. You can persuade people into agreeing on several topics, and thus create a level of influence; and once you have influence, it becomes easier to persuade. It's a vicious circle.

### Rapport

In order to build influence, you need to develop a certain degree of rapport with the prospect. The greater your rapport, the greater your ability to influence. Rapport happens when we identify with someone in some way. There are two main methods of gaining rapport, these are:
***1. Identification:*** Identification happens when we

recognize someone else as being similar to ourselves. The more someone appears to be just like us, the more we like and trust them. **2. *Internalization:*** Internalization happens when we agree with another person's beliefs and behavior, both internally and publically. I call this the Superman effect... You can admire someone else's beliefs and actions, almost to the degree that you would like to be just like them (How could anybody not want to be like Superman?).

Identification is easier to establish. This was briefly discussed in chapter three. The more you can identify yourself with your prospect, through your words, speech and actions, the greater the degree of rapport, both on a conscious and an unconscious level. Knowing this explains a lot about how I chose my friends in school... When I was in high-school, all the students segmented themselves into groups. The cool kids with the cool kids, the nerds with the nerds, and the average with the average. The kids in my school were able to seek out and identify with others who dressed the same, talked the same, used the same lingo, acted similar, had the same interests and hobbies, and so on. The same thing happened in university, and the same thing happened after that. I think its universal!

## Basic Relationship Skills

In order to gain good rapport with your prospect, you need to incorporate some basic relationship skills: By "basic" I mean you need to be friendly, have a good personality, generally be in a good mood, and be supportive of those you choose to associate with (and those who choose to associate with you). Nobody wants to be around friends who are negative, depressing or condescending all (or most) of the time. Build additional rapport by perfecting your ability to make others feel good about you, and about themselves. When you can do this effectively, people will become attracted to you – like a magnet.

**Be Interested In Your Prospects**

Begin by showing interest in the other person... I noticed in high-school - A boy and a girl could sit directly beside each other and never notice the other existed... But when one of the two had learned that the other was interested in them, they began to develop an interest in that other person also. The same thing happens throughout life... When we show sincere interest in our prospects, they will be more likely to develop a sincere interest in us.

The easiest way to show deep interest in other people is simply to listen to their concerns, and give suggestions when warranted. Another method is to ask inquisitive questions that give the perception that you want to know more. Finally, you can simply say good things about the person, especially in front of others.

**Focus On Them First**

My first blind date was a total blunder. We (me and my blind date) met a really nice restaurant, which was supposed to be the start a beautiful night. I had arrived first and was waiting at the door. We both entered the restaurant, waited to be seated, and finally sat down at a table. There was a beautiful rose in the center of the table... Music in the background... Lights lit dimly... It was a gorgeous setting. Then... I began to talk... I started talking about all of the things that I was interested in... Of course,

I asked her opinion on many things, I told her about my childhood, my interests, my dreams, and then I started talking about what I would like to do for the remainder of the night... I guess I was trying to keep her interested in me, trying not to be boring. Half way through dinner my date stood up, and said "Call me when you're not so in-to yourself"... And walked out the door.

That was my first lesson about courtship (dating). The lesson - It's all about her... When you want to start a relationship with someone, any relationship... it's all about them. Begin by putting all focus on the other person (change your words and phrases to sound like they are focused on them), and eventually... They will begin to return the favor, and in no time the relationship will develop more equally. At this point, a level of rapport begins to grow as a reciprocity of personal interest begins to develop.

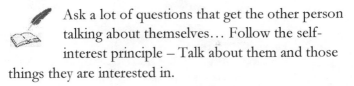

Ask a lot of questions that get the other person talking about themselves... Follow the self-interest principle – Talk about them and those things they are interested in.

**Use Their Name**

People are immediately attracted to their own name. We are conditioned throughout our lives to pay attention when someone calls out our name. When you use someone's name, it creates a sense of familiarity (where they perceive that they know you, or that you know them), at least for a split second.

When you can use a person's first name (as oppose to their family name), it creates an even deeper sense of familiarity. Be cautious though, not to use a person's name too often as they may become irritated with its overuse. You may even want to do the polite thing, and ask them for permission to use their first name.

**Mirroring and Matching**

Mirroring and matching is about showing that you and your prospect are alike. As mentioned earlier, the more you show similarities between yourself and your prospect, the more they like, and trust you. This is because, unconsciously, they like and trust themselves, and therefore, if you are just like them, they must also like and trust you. Mirroring means if your prospect performs some action, you follow by performing the same action, but not necessarily exactly the same (Perhaps in reverse order, using the opposite side of the body, etc.). Matching means if your prospect performs an action in some specified way, you perform the action in the same way. When we consciously (As oppose to unconsciously) become similar to our prospects, we have more control over the development of rapport in this manner.

You can mirror or match just about anything the other person does... And the more you apply this, the greater the level of rapport. One word of caution though, don't be so obvious that the other person realizes you are mirroring and matching them on purpose - As this will have a reverse effect. Sometimes it is necessary to give a short delay before applying mirroring and matching techniques - Anywhere from 3 to 5 seconds should be fine.

Some of the things you can mirror and match include: Breathing; use of key words or sentences; vocal style (pace, volume, tone, etc.); major body movements; minor body movements; micro-expressions; style of handshake; emotion; or just about anything else noticeable about the other person.

## Develop Influence

In order to develop influence, you need to have the type of persona that your prospects will appreciate. "Persona" is the way in which the outside world perceives you - Their interpretation of you as a person. Remember, that in everything you do, every moment of your life, people are making judgments about you. You also have to develop a personality that other people will appreciate, which means you need to be kind, patient and confident.

### Values & Beliefs

Values help us define what is right and wrong, while beliefs help us create our perception of existence… What is, and what is not. Once people have developed values and beliefs, they become very unyielding in terms of changing those values and beliefs. Entire organizations, religious and otherwise, have been established based on the sharing of common values and beliefs.

Values are learned and developed from the days of our childhood. As we age, we also learn new values that replace old ones. As we mature, we may develop new values based on our understanding of right and wrong, which may have been shared by authority figures, family and peers, or by people we respect and/or admire (I learned mine by watching Superman cartoons).

Beliefs are enclosed in memory, repetition and credibility of the source. We establish our perception of existence based on what we know to be true, through our own past experience and the shared experiences of others whom we trust. Some beliefs may also be formed through desire – For instance: Many people believe in God, though there is no proof or credible source to his existence... But the desire to acknowledge something bigger than ourselves gives us a sense of security and a definitive place in the world.

Since it is difficult to simply change a person's values and beliefs, it makes sense then, if you want to change a person's actions and attitude, to begin by creating a direct association between the actions and attitude you want them to undertake, and the values and beliefs they already have. In short, if you want to move people, begin from where they are.

**Trust**

Trust is probably the most important factor to consider in developing influence. When people trust you, they will believe you, and they are most likely to follow you. Without trust, there truly is no REAL relationship.

Trust, however, exists on different levels. It may be useful to gauge how much your prospects and customers trust you, and on which aspects.

There are several factors that will affect the level of trust someone has for you, some of which are: ***1. Predictability:*** Being able to predict how people will behave helps us feel secure. ***2. Reliability:*** Over time, when we are perceived as being reliable under particular circumstances, a level of trust occurs, and a belief that we will continue to be reliable under similar circumstances. ***3. Reciprocity:*** When someone does us a favor, they (usually) expect that we will be willing to return a similar favor under similar circumstances. **4. Active and Passive Care:** When people recognize that we care about them, and act out of their best interest, or otherwise act in a caring manner, the level of rapport, and thus trust, significantly increases.

Your prospect's perception of your predictability and reliability are gained through time, in both major and minor matters – While it is important to remain predictable and reliable with major matters, even small things such as timely follow-ups or sending emails at regular intervals will greatly enhance their perception of both predictability and reliability – And thus also the level of trust.

## Persuasion

Persuasive communication uses a variety of emotive language, logic and reasoning and hypnotic suggestion, in such a way as to gain the prospect's agreement and motivate the prospect into acting on his own free will.

### Two Routes To Persuasion

There are essentially two routes to persuasion. The first route, called The Central Route, involves the use of (perceived) logic, to persuade the prospect that one choice is more logical than another. The choice you want your prospect to proceed with does not necessarily have to be the logical choice, as long as your prospect perceives it as being the logical choice. One of the best methods of communicating logic can be found in Rhetoric, which was originally developed by Aristotle in the 4th century. The second route to persuasion, called the Peripheral Route, involves employing your prospects emotions to persuade him (which we have previously spent some time discussing).

While it is possible to persuade somebody to do something by using either of the two, the central route or the peripheral route, alone (logic or emotion), its most effective to use both of these routes in progressive succession. Remember, people make that final buying decision emotionally, and then justify that decision with logic… Depending on the type of personality that you're attempting to persuade, either begin with emotion, move to logic, and then return to emotion (energetic and amiable personalities); or by beginning with logic, moving the prospect emotionally, and reinserting logic (analytic and driver personalities).

## Factors of Persuasion

There are a variety of factors that can aid in the type of, and level of, persuasiveness that can be attained. Persuasion can be direct, indirect or covert. While direct persuasion is straight-forward in its communication; indirect persuasion uses a more subtle approach, employing suggestions, and allowing the prospect to make the final decision. Covert persuasion is designed not to be recognized at all, allowing the prospect to believe the idea was completely his, and is the most difficult to attain. The following paragraphs summarize 7 principles of persuasion reported by Dr. Robert Cialdini, a foremost expert in persuasion and influence:

## Authority

There are two types of authority that can be considered in persuasion: The authority that comes from rank or positioning, such as that of an officer of the law; and the authority that is granted by being an expert in a specific field (thus comes the saying "he's an authority on the subject of…"). If either enough people, or the right people, perceive you as being an expert, you can gain more credibility as an authority.

People tend to trust the advice and decisions of those who are perceived as an authority, regardless of the type of authority the person is perceived as having (by rank or by degree of experience).

Authority can be established or perceived, whereas established authority has been earned, and perceived authority is believed to be existing, even if no proof has been provided. An example of perceived authority would be the wearing of uniforms – When a person wears a particular uniform, we presume that person has the authority generally given to one who wears such a uniform, regardless of any additional proof. The same thing happens through the use of speech – When a person speaks in a deep and commanding tone, there is a generally assumption that he has authority to do so; additionally, when a person uses the terminology and language common to a particular field of study, and appears to have more knowledge than ourselves, we tend to believe that he is (to varying degrees) somewhat of an authority on the topic.

 Be cautious of how authority can be gained, and realize that authority can also be lost in a similar fashion!

**Liking**

The more someone likes you, the more they are willing to do for you in return for your friendship; and the more they are willing to trust you. When we recognize that someone likes us, we are more apt to like them in return. People are also more likely to accept new ideas, and follow someone whom they know, like and trust. If you can get a person admire in you in some way, the effect is amplified.

Don't forget to remind people that you care about them. Joe Girard built his career largely in part by having constantly reminded be that he cared about them and liked them. You can do the same! You phrases such as "I care about you"; "I appreciate having you as a customer and a friend"; "I like you"; or "I enjoy your company". When you make such statements in front of others, the effect is amplified.

**Commitment**

Once people commit to something, they generally prefer to see it through. One reason is the effect of cognitive dissonance - People generally like to act in a manner that is congruent with what they say, and when their words and their actions don't align, people feel bad about themselves. Another reason is that people don't want to let other's down, as this causes other people to see them in a negative view.

Most people are not likely to give you their full commitment, unless a preferred relationship has been previously established. They may, however, be willing to give minor commitments. Each consecutive minor commitment you can gain will bring your prospect closer to a major commitment... This is a key often used by seduction artists – They gain minor commitments until full commitment is gained.

The opposite also holds true... If you can get people to commit to a larger purchase, asking them to commit to minor purchases is much easier. When I bought my first car, it came with a stock stereo and stock equipment. The salesperson first gained my full commitment on buying the car, and then followed through by getting me to purchase all the bells and whistles such as a DVD player, reclining seats and so on.

## Consistency

While it is true that people seek variation in life in order to keep things interesting, people rely heavily on great degrees of consistency. Having certain things remain the same, gives us a sense of security *(Maslow's second hierarchy)* and stability; as well as a sense of understanding and (perhaps) familiarity. When aspects of our life are often inconsistent, we perceive this is as chaotic and unreliable, and (most likely) confusing.

Imagine if your wife or spouse behaved differently from day to day... Or if your best friend had multiple personalities. What would your boss say if you showed up at work whenever you felt like it? The lack of consistency would surely cause elevated levels of stress and anxiety, a normal response to unfamiliar situations.

 Consistency and commitment work hand in hand. Get people to make small commitments that are consistent in nature. Remind them of their consistent nature when you want them to continue being consistent.

## Reciprocity

When someone does a favor for us, we are more likely to be compelled to do a favor for them. This could be because of a perceived state of "debt" or it could be because we want to believe that we are good in nature, and fair to others, and so will attempt to return a favor whether or not we are asked to, in order to avoid cognitive dissonance.

Studies have shown that when one person does a small favor for another, the favor is likely to be returned in greater value... Almost as if the favor is being returned "with interest". This may occur because of a need to remain in power within a developing relationship; or it could possibly be due to the fear of being in future debt if/when additional favors are performed.

The Perfect Sales Pro will use the power of reciprocity as much as possible. Remember that reciprocity is a social response, meaning that if the receiver of a favor perceives the favor was performed for the sole purpose of asking for something in return, the effect is lost, so you perform a favor for your prospect, do not ask for a favor in return immediately.

## Consensus *(The Bandwagon Effect)*

Consensus is often referred to as the "bandwagon effect", or "group-thinking". Consensus happens when other people agree on a particular subject or idea. The term bandwagon effect became popular after a political campaign by former entertainer Dan Rice in the 1800's, who used a band-wagon (a popular item for circus entertainers at the time) in his political campaign... As more and more people started to join his campaign in aspiration of piggy-backing on success, the term "jump on the band-wagon" was developed to refer to people who associate themselves with something without knowing or considering what they are associating themselves with.

When people notice that others are doing something, they tend to assume that others must know something of value that they don't. When the number of people who agree on a particular subject grows, there is a tendency to think "so many people couldn't possibly be wrong!"

The Perfect Sales Pro will use consensus by showing the prospect others who have purchased the product. The more influential those "others" are, the greater its power (influential to the prospect, that is).

Consensus can be real or it can be perceived: for example, in the use of words such as "many people like yourself have purchased…" or "We just sold to your top three competitors!" When I use to sell door-to-door, I would fill out several 'sell-sheets" prior to the start of the day with bogus information, and flip through those pages as the next prospect opened the door, just to leave the impression that many people have already purchased. Perception is key!

### Scarcity

Generally, the less of something that exists (such as money or gold), the more valuable it is. The value of any particular thing can also be attributed to supply and demand. Thus, something becomes more valuable when the demand is high and the supply is low. It is these ideas that define scarcity... Scarcity occurs when people want something, but there is only a limited amount of it- And when this happens, it becomes even more valuable (or in some cases, it is only 'perceived' as more valuable).

There are many things that you can make scarce, or at the least leave an impression of scarcity. These include: Specials and savings (i.e. for the first 100 purchases only!); as well as your personal time (if you can make yourself valuable enough to your prospects).

## Additional Persuasive Techniques

Throughout this book, we have discussed many techniques that aid in the persuasive process: From self-development (persona, confidence, etc.) to consumer psychology (personality types, motivation and buying psychology); from effective communication (choice words, body language, etc.) to targeting the right prospects; and from presentations (AIDA, features and benefits, etc.) to sales (questions, objection handling and closing) and persuasion techniques. In the next chapter, we will also discuss relationship skills, which also contribute to persuasion. Below, are a few additional considerations when attempting to persuade:

### Agreement

The Perfect Sales Pro will gain persuasive momentum through agreement. The more your prospect agrees with you on minor points, the more he is likely to agree with you on the major point (the buying decision). This concept employs the use of commitment... How could the prospect possibly disagree on the buying decision when he has agreed on everything else leading to that decision.

A short word of caution here: The reverse also holds true... The more your prospect disagrees with you, the less likely he will make a buying decision. Disagreement also creates emotional friction as the prospect recognizes that you and he are not alike. Avoid ALL emotional friction!!!

## Pre-Thanking

Traditionally, we thank people for having done something after they have done it. Thus, thanking them concludes the act of having done it. This mentality has been engraved in most of us. By thanking your prospect in advance, they are more likely to complete the action.

## Information Manipulation

Don't be too ready to tell everybody everything. Be conscious about the amount of information you provide people. Information manipulation is about withholding information, or providing information, depending on how it best suits your needs.

You can withhold important or valuable information in order to direct the prospect's thought pattern in one direction or another, or possibly to drive curiosity. You can prevent the prospect from having all the information necessary to make his own decision (making him dependent on you). You can also overload the prospect with information to establish yourself as a credible authority (this works especially well if you provide technical, specific or little-known information).

# Reframing

People make decisions based on their understanding of a particular thing, and the meaning that they associate to it. Reframing involves changing meaning, and thus their understanding of something, in order to persuade them to your point of view.

A classic example of reframing can be found in the story of the Ugly Duckling. The story tells of a homely little duck, born in a barnyard who suffers abuse from the other duck's around him, but the ugly duckling was never really a duck at all... After a lonely winter, he matures into a beautiful swan. The perception of whether he was ugly or beautiful was dependent on whether he was viewed as a baby duck or a baby swan. Had he had been raised with a family of swan's (and not ducks) he would not have been ridiculed.

In the 1984 U.S. presidential campaign, Ronald Reagan ran against Walter Mondale. Reagan was 73 years old, which was considered much older than any other sitting presidents before him, and was under pressure when this was viewed as an issue in the campaign. When he was asked about it bluntly in the second debate, Reagan answered: *"I want you to know that also I will not make age an issue of this campaign. I am not going to exploit, for political purposes, my opponent's youth and inexperience."* - A perfect example of reframing! Reagan didn't see himself as old, he saw himself as experienced.

Reframing, thus, involves changing the words, phrases, ideas and associations that are used, in order to change the meaning of something. There are several ways to do this: ***1. Use similar words*** (such as synonyms - i.e. <u>cost</u> vs. <u>investment</u>); ***2. Use related concepts*** (i.e. estimated <u>time</u> of arrival vs. estimated <u>distance</u>). ***3. Use contrasting concepts*** (glass <u>half empty</u> vs. glass <u>half full</u>).

In my days of selling windows for a national window and door company, I came across an intriguing prospect whom I found to be very difficult to work with. He began by remarking how our windows were more expensive than competitive windows… I replied by saying "yes sir, they are priced a little higher than most other windows, but over a term of 5-10 years, the total cost of windows diminishes and the windows pay for themselves. You see sir, these are the highest energy efficient windows available, and are certain to lower your home heating bills dramatically". This was a perfect example of reframing using similar words – rather than focus on the upfront <u>price</u>, I focused on the long-term <u>cost</u>.

As we continued talking the prospect complained about the time it would take to have a set of windows delivered to his home. I told him "It may take a few extra days sir, this is because we take special pride in our service and we check everything to make sure you are getting the best possible windows, and the best possible service". Here, I used a similar concept to reframe time of arrival with care and quality of service.

The prospect continued by stating he appreciated all the information that I've provided him so far, but unfortunately would not be able to purchase the windows due to a conflict between his current budget and the higher price point of the windows. I replied "sir, if you're serious about owning these quality windows, you now have a great opportunity to take advantage of our no-interest payment option. Here, I used a contrasting concept to reframe an unfortunate conflict into an opportunity. Oh… And the prospect DID buy the windows.

## Logic & Emotion

All persuasion is made effective through the proper use of logic and emotion. This is true whether it be verbally, written or non-verbal.

Our brains are primarily made up of two halves, the left and right hemisphere. These two halves are each responsible for a different set of processing. The left hemisphere of the brain is responsible for most of our logic and reasoning; while the right hemisphere of the brain is mostly responsible for our creative and emotional processing. These two halves of the brain, in most of us, have trouble operating simultaneously. This means that as a person processes more logic, their level of emotion is reduced; and (more importantly in sales persuasion) the more they process thoughts creatively or emotionally, the greater the reduction in their processing of logic and reasoning.

In most people, one hemisphere of the brain is more predominant. Think back to our four characteristics or interpersonal styles (Chapter 2): Drivers and Analytics have a stronger left hemisphere; while the Energetic and Amiable type have a stronger right hemisphere. Thus, reducing logic by raising emotion is much easier with Energetic and Amiable type personalities.

**Logic**

Logic gives us a basis for reasoning with our prospects. There are four major forms of logic: **1. Syllogistic Reasoning:** Interpreting the "truth" of one thing based on its relationship or association with something else (i.e. blue berries are good for you, thus all berries must be good for you – not necessarily true!). **2. Deductive Reasoning:** Using the final accomplishment, and working backward to prove something involved was true (This is how murder mysteries are solved). **3. Inductive Reasoning:** Establishing facts, and assembling those facts to prove the existence of something (the opposite of deductive reasoning). **4. Abductive Reasoning:** Assuming that two things are connected without proof, often based on some common understanding (i.e. If I don't say hello to you, then I must be angry with you).

As an example: When using Syllogistic Reasoning to persuade someone to buy insurance, you may say: "One out of four people need insurance when they least expect it *(the association)*… Say, you have four people in your household don't you? *(The syllogism)*… Chances are one of you will need insurance when least expected… Don't you feel it would better to buy <u>before</u> that happens? *(The close)*"

Review the types of logic above and discover the many different ways you could incorporate them into your sales presentation.

**Emotion**

People make decisions based on desire, or emotional need. Every human action, thus, is performed for the purpose of benefiting the person acting in some way. There are many forms of benefit that one can aim to achieve, this can be briefly found in Maslow's Hierarchy (chapter 2). A person may, for example, forgo physical benefits (such as money or belongings), for benefits gained through self-actualization (such as self-perception, future potential or personal growth).

The funny thing about emotion is... People are likely to react to you, the same way that you act toward them. Meaning, if you portray emotion toward someone, they will likely respond with the same or similar emotion. This is called "emotional contagion".

To begin persuading someone of something, begin by determining where the prospect is, meaning - evaluate what values they have, what beliefs they hold, and whether they are predominantly emotional or logical (so define their personality style). Remember - It is much easier to move your prospect to your point of view in smaller steps, than in one full leap.

 For those who are predominantly logical (Driver and Analytic type), begin with a logically sound reason to buy, then drive their level of emotion. For those who are predominantly emotional (Energetic and Amiable type), begin by stirring up their emotional reasons to buy, then add some bit of logic. I personally like to move people through three fluctuating states, as follows:

For predominantly logical personalities: Logic ➡ Emotion ➡ Logic.

For predominantly emotional personalities: Emotion ➡ Logic ➡ Emotion

# Negotiations

Negotiations is a part of persuasion and sales. It involves giving in to the other person's view, so that they may give in to your point of view, so that agreement may be reached and the sale may be closed.

## Reluctance to Negotiate

Regardless of the logical need for negotiation and the effect of cooperation in reaching a fair and mutually-beneficial agreement, most people still do not like to engage in negotiation, and many would even opt to avoid the situation all-together if it involves negotiating. This is true because of two main reasons: ***1. Biological / Emotional Reasons:*** Negotiation often triggers anxiety as neurochemicals are released into the brain, most often forcing a fight-or-flight response. ***2. Psychological / Social Reasons:*** We often view the adversary of a negotiation as an "enemy", rather than simply as an individual with different views, and this in turn triggers a series of negative feelings toward that individual

Prior to entering into negotiation, consider each of these factors and how they may affect both your negotiation strategy and that of the other person.

## Factors in Negotiation

There are several factors that affect the outcome of a negotiation, as well as the way in which the negotiation takes place. Some of these include: ***1. Power:*** The power that one person has over the other, and the way in which that person is able to influence the other party. There are many forms of power, such as authority, status, and position. ***2. Time:*** The less time one has to negotiate, the more quickly they are in need of making a decision. This puts them at a disadvantage, especially if the other party is not in so much of a hurry. ***3. Commitment:*** The more committed one side is to accomplishing a successful negotiation, the more likely they will be to compromise. Additionally, as mentioned earlier... Minor commitments can also be employed as a persuasion strategy. ***4. Risk:*** Negotiations hold risks for both sides... both immediate and future risks. The more risks involved, the more likely a person will want to negotiate in their own favor, as appose to seeking a fair result (risks are thus perceived as potential costs). **5. Relationships:** The degree to which the two parties have established a relationship can effect both the outcome of the negotiation as well as the way in which the negotiation takes place.

**Negotiation Tactics:**

Over the past few thousand years, good negotiators have developed several tactics to effectively deal with such situations. Some of those include: ***1. The 'Take It or Leave It':*** Provide your final offer, and be willing to walk away if it is not accepted. ***2. The Bogey:*** An unwavering offer is given, and a third party (such as a superior) is the reason no further concessions may be made. ***3. The Crunch:*** This is where one party uses a "You've got to do better than that" attitude. It is essentially a form of the "Take It or Leave It" tactic. ***4. Stating Benefits / Problems:*** By stating the benefits, and the value associated with those benefits (related to your point of view) you can often win a negotiation. Conversely, you can state the problems, and the costs associated with those problems (related to the other person's point of view).

The Perfect Sales Pro understands the importance of reputation and relationships, and will therefore strive for a win-win negotiation as often as possible, even when gaining the higher advantage.

You can learn more about negotiation skills in The Master Sales Manual, and subsequent books.

# Concept #9
# Build Powerful Relationships

*I*t's important to understand that ANY association between two people is effectively a relationship. Most relationships are supported by some mutual level of interdependence, which means that on some level, the two (or more) people within the relationship depend on each other. This dependency may not necessarily be for life's needs and necessities, but rather for those things that cannot readily be measured, such as acquisition of Maslow's higher level needs (friendship, love and belonging, social needs, development of self-esteem, self-actualization, etc.). Two predominant relationship theories are Wheel theory and Social Exchange theory *(other relationship theories can be found in my next book: The Master Sales Manual)*:

## Wheel Theory

Psychologists and sociologists have long sought to understand relationships and the way in which they are formed, and there are many theories to suggest how this is done. One of the predominant theories of relationship development is the Wheel Theory proposed by Sociologist Ira Reiss. This theory suggests that relationships progress through a series of four basic stages: ***1. Rapport:*** Basic rapport is developed between the two individuals. ***2. Self-Revelation:*** Each party begins to disclose more information about oneself to other. ***3. Mutual Dependency:*** Each party in the relationship begins to depend on the other, for one thing or another. ***4. Intimacy Need Fulfillment:*** Each party in the relationship evaluates whether the other can fulfill the basic need for intimacy on some level, which may be friendship, on-going business relationship, or lovers).

Get others to disclose more and more about themselves, as an exchange of reciprocity… Give a little bit about yourself in exchange for a little more about them. Create dependency by gradually growing the frequency of contact – The more you become a part of someone's "life", the more they become dependent on that level of consistency, and negative feelings may occur if that consistency is lost. Create situations for the relationship to become more intimate, including physical contact (not necessarily sexual in nature), mutual cooperation toward shared goals, and leisure activity (such as golfing).

**Social Exchange**

In the 1950's, American Sociologist George Homans studied how people view relationships as a social exchange. He claimed that people make decisions about relationships based on their assessment of cost vs. value. When a relationship begins to cost too much, people begin considering whether there is value in remaining in the relationship.

Find out what others consider valuable within a relationship, and ensure that you are providing more value than the perceived cost of continuing the relationship.

## Building The Relationship

You can build or break a relationship in just a few simple steps. Few people are conscious about the way in which they act and interact within a relationship. Below we will discuss a few things that you can do pro-actively to build a relationship in your favor:

**Investment**

In the previous chapter we discussed building rapport, and how rapport is developed when we either identify with, or internalize with somebody. You may have thought… "But I have friends I don't identify or internalize with?" If you think back to when you met, chances are most likely that you did at that time, thus allowing the relationship to develop to a point where you have invested a certain degree of time and effort to validate continuing the relationship. People consider time and effort as cost… And thus seek to gain from that time and effort. As we discussed earlier, relationships are allowed (by both parties) to develop because we expect, in some way, that those relationship will give more value than they cost, thus the time and effort involved in developing and sustaining a relationship is viewed as an investment. As in accounting, when we invest time in a relationship that we do not benefit from, we often think of it as a sort of "sunk cost".

It is safe to say that most people do not like to lose. It is for this reason that relationships, even if they become costly, are sustained in the hopes of future gain. Even to the degree that we may attempt to change others into becoming what we want them to be, though most often to no avail.

**Value**

People seek a certain degree of value in their relationships. The amount of value must surpass the cost of sustaining the relationship. The more value that we find in a particular relationship the more we are drawn to that relationship – This is our inherent need to gain pleasure in life… The more pleasure we gain from something, the more we are drawn toward it and the more we <u>want</u> to gain pleasure from it.

As a simple example: Imagine yourself walking into your local coffee shop… You stand in line and finally get to the counter where you order a large coffee with two cream and two sugar. The counterperson fills your order, and hands it to you – Immediately yelling "next person please!" While you enjoy your cup of coffee, your experience was nothing more than average. Now replay the situation, but as your standing in line, the counterperson simply smiles at you – She doesn't know you and you don't know her. You get to the counter and order a large coffee with two cream and two sugar, and the counterperson asks "do you live around here?" You answer "No, but I work down the street"… And the counterperson replies by asking for your name, and then saying "I'll try to remember your order the next time you come in… Enjoy the coffee and I hope you have a great day!" The second experience with that counterperson made you feel good. You're not just another person coming into just another coffee shop. You're more likely to return to that coffee shop instead of going to one down the street, simply because of the personal pleasure you gained from the "now developing" relationship with that counterperson. You would probably learn her name too, and seek small conversation the next few times you walk in… Why? Because it makes you feel good.

**The Ben Franklin Effect:**

Ben Franklin, one of the founding fathers of the United States, was a master at building relationships. One of the basic methods that Franklin used to gain the friendship of others was to ask for their help in something. His theory was that people only do favors for those they consider a friend. When you do a favor for another person, it also puts you in a position of power and superiority, at least regarding that task or situation – We all like to feel powerful and important.

This is a tactic you should try to incorporate often. Even small favors provide great results. When trying to develop a relationship, incorporate wording such as "Can I ask you a (small) favor?" Or "Can you help me (for a moment)?"

**Contact Hypothesis**

When people come together under certain circumstances, such as facing common difficulties, or working toward a common goal, a bond is created that helps the relationship flourish. The degree of importance in the goal, the amount of time spent working on it, and the degree of closeness in which people work together, often have an impact on the development of the relationship. The importance of the goal has the same effect even when it is only "perceived" as being important – The same holds true for the degree of closeness.

I know a very successful insurance salesman who approaches every customer by first explaining to them how important their choice of insurance is, and follows this by repeatedly suggesting "Don't worry, we'll work together through this to make sure that you have the best coverage at the best value". Rather than saying "I'm here to help you" (which puts the salesman in a position of power and the customer at a lesser position), he states "I'm here to work with you". The choice of words dramatically changes the context of the entire conversation.

This often works also when two individual goals are sought and two people work towards them together. I was once in a position (a long time ago) where I had little money, and lived at a hostile. Unlike most of the people there, I worked very hard to quickly excel into a more favorable situation. I found one other individual there who worked as hard as I did, though followed a different path. We vowed to help each other succeed from there on, and developed a powerful relationship. Although we were two different people on two different paths, and had two separate goals that were only united by the common desire to succeed, the effects of contact hypothesis took place.

**The Dilution Effect**

Common ideas, such as stereotypes, can be diluted or even eliminated when additional information is provided about a person. For example: Many people stereotype all sales people as being "snake oil artists", willing to cheat, lie and steal to get the sale... But when information about a specific sales person is provided, especially in the form of testimonials or stories, that sales person begins to be judged by his individualism, rather than his association with the sales profession.

The great thing about the dilution effect, is that it often works regardless of the 'source' of the additional information. However, when that information is provided by an outside source, the effect is stronger… And even stronger yet when the source is perceived as being close to receiver.

You can take advantage of the dilution effect by telling stories about yourself (even short or brief stories), about how you have worked with other prospects or customers. If you want a stronger effect, get someone else to tell the story. If you can get someone who is close to your prospect in some way, the effect is even stronger yet.

## Familiarity & The Mere Exposure Effect

Psychologists have performed several tests to prove how the more we are exposed to a particular thing (such as people, places, objects or ideas), the more we begin to like it or appreciate it. This is not to say that people will eventually begin to prefer one thing over another, but simply to dislike it less. In relationships, sociologists have shown how familiarity is one of the key factors in the development of relationships. These concepts often work in unison with many of the other concepts related to the development of relationships, such as the need for predictability, certainty and reliability.

Familiarity and mere exposure often do not consistently require direct contact. People think in terms of images. When we create an image of ourselves in the mind of another person, we trigger these principles. Joe Girard, the only salesperson ever to be inducted into the Guinness book of world record, would find out as much information as he could about his customers (a little at a time), and send them Christmas cards, birthday cards, etc. His goal was to become a family household name – allowing the principles of familiarity and mere exposure to take effect.

## Emotional Involvement

People want and seek to experience emotional involvement in a relationship. Specifically, people seek to experience those emotions that make them feel good - Good about themselves, and good about their involvement in the relationship. Typically, the more you can make people feel good, the more the relationship advances - The reverse is true when you make people feel badly. It's also important to realize that different people will seek a different level of emotional involvement, but that's too large of a topic to be covered in this book.

## Customer Service Skills

In today's world, consumers have become much more demanding than they were in the past. Today, customers require a level of service... before, during and after the sale... And they already have an idea as to what level of service they expect. Below, I've attempted to include a few of the most important techniques in customer service.

### Smile

Remember that people are making judgments about you every moment of your life. They judge what type of person you are, as well as what type of mood you're in. Smiling gives a good impression about you... It suggests that you're a pleasant individual and / or that you're in a good mood. Also remember that people tend to move toward pleasant experiences and away from unpleasant experiences. Lack of smiling may make you unapproachable.

## Respect

People have a natural tendency to treat others the way that they are treated… To react to others in a similar manner in which people act toward them. Begin all your relationships with respect, and carry that respect throughout the term of the relationship, and people are likely to do the same with you.

## Listen Attentively, Don't Interrupt

Listening to what people have to say with complete attention, shows that you are interested in the conversation. When you interrupt people, it is a sign of disrespect, and suggests that what they have to say is not important to you (possibly suggesting that what you have to do or say is more important). There are times when you may need to interrupt to keep the conversation on track, but judge this carefully.

## Tell Them Why

People are always wondering why. I would almost suggest that "Why" is the magic question… If you can't answer it, nothing else matters. When you find yourself in a position where you cannot assist your customers, or cannot provide them with the results they want, tell them why.

People are very quick to ask why something cannot be done the way they expect it to, and they often allow themselves to become irritated, frustrated or angry rather quickly. The Perfect Sales Pro will answer "why" before stating that you cannot perform the action they request. An example of this would be "Our new policies do not allow us to give discounts (the why),

I'm sorry but I will not be able to lower the cost of this product" (the statement).

## Don't Argue - Agree

Arguing creates emotional friction. It eliminates cooperation, dissolves rapport, and separates you from the prospect. When building relationships you want to generate as little emotional friction between yourself and the prospect (or customer) as possible. When you agree with the prospect, you show that you and he are alike, and are also likeminded.

Even when you disagree with the prospect (or customer), you can begin your statement by, at the very least, agreeing that the prospect (or customer) is entitled to his opinion. Use statements similar to "I can see where you're coming from, you may also want to consider…" or "I understand what you're saying, do you think possibly…"

## Focus On The Positive

Always direct the customer's attention toward the positive things. Don't focus on what you can't do, but what you can do. You want to eliminate as much opportunity for the customer to have a negative experience as possible. For example, don't simply say "We can't do that",… Rather say "Although we can't do that, what we can do is…" or something to that effect.

## Show Them You Care

People are driven toward others, when they honestly believe that other person cares about them. This is Maslow's third stage in the hierarchy, we all need to be loved. Use empathy to show people that you care about them. Listen attentively to what they have to say. Finally, try to help them solve their issues, even if only by suggesting how they can do so themselves.

## Working With Angry Customers

Remember earlier, we suggested that the human brain processes emotion and logic in contrasting fashion - So when emotion rises, logic declines; and vice-versa. When customers call you or come to you with a complaint... They are acting emotionally, and therefore, before you can begin to deal with their situation, you must first resolve the emotion.

The worst thing you could do when a customer is angry, is to reply with retaliating anger. We suggested earlier that people (generally) will react to you in the same manner that you act toward them (a theory called "emotional contagion"), thus becoming angry with a customer who is already in a state of anger, can only lead in the wrong direction.

### Lowering The Emotional State

A better solution is to either allow the customer to release the anger or frustration that they are experiencing by giving them a moment to express themselves - Once customers are provided the opportunity to express themselves, they are generally more open to reasonable discussion.

Another solution is to cause the customer to begin thinking with logic (thus lowering the emotional state). There are many ways to cause a customer to lower emotion by activating the logical hemisphere of the brain... Probably the easiest method of doing this, is to put the customer into a problem-solving state by asking him to provide solutions for his own issues. Such questions may include "I'm sorry that this has occurred, what can we do to resolve this for you?" or "I apologize for the inconvenience, we can do __A__ or __B__. Which would you prefer?"

## Promote Cooperation

Promote cooperation with the customer through an understanding of their situation, and possibly even through agreeing with them on some points. If you can also get them to agree with you on some points, the effect is amplified.

## Be The Customer's Advocate

The more your customer's see you as a friend, rather than just an employee of the company, the more open they will be to your suggestions, and the more likely they will seek cooperation with you. One way of achieving this is by providing the perception that you are willing to do everything you can do assist the customer, and revert the blame to the company, or its procedures and regulations (or any higher power). Again, since perception is key here, you may even want to give the customer the impression that you have gone to speak with upper management on their behalf. The more the customer believes that you are their friend, and you are on their side... The more they will work with you.

## Confirm The Resolution

If you have come to an agreement with the customer on a resolution, get the customer to confirm the resolution with you. The more your resolution appears to be the customer's idea, the more satisfied they will be with that resolution.

## Social Networking

Social networking is about meeting people through people. It is a form of leverage that allows you to find more prospects with less work. The idea combines a couple of proven theories - first, warm leads (prospects whom you know directly or whom you can be introduced to through someone you know) are more likely to buy from you than cold leads (prospects who don't know you). Second, the more people you know, the more likely you are to find warm leads. In addition to this, you can expect that people who like you, will refer their friends and colleagues to you whenever those friends and colleagues are searching for a product that you offer.

You see how social networking - online (on the internet) or offline (in the real world) is very important to salespeople. Not everybody, though, is going to give your social network the same degree of leverage. Certain types of individuals can provide you more leverage than others. You want to seek people who are more sociable; have large followings or groups of friends; are involved in activities that involve large groups; or hold a great amount of influence amongst their peers. Building relationships with these people will allow you to take advantage of the pre-existing leverage that these folks hold.

 Learn to categorize the people in your network according the amount of leverage that they provide you. Relationships require a great amount of time and energy, so spend the most amount of time and energy with those people who provide you with the most leverage or the greatest amount of return on your investment.

You can learn more about relationship skills in The Master Sales Manual, and subsequent books.

# Concept #10
# Grow Your Business

The final step in the process is to look for ways to keep your business growing. After closing the sale and providing customer service. Beyond self-marketing and growing your network. Now, you can find ways to keep your existing customers, and find other markets to sell to.

## Increase Customer Participation

The first step in your growth plan is to begin with your existing customers. While it's nice to close a sale with a customer, you should want to build a great relationship with that customer, so that when he chooses to purchase another product that you sell, he will also buy from you.

The Perfect Sales Pro will begin is by creating a detailed understanding of new and existing customers. Maybe you have different categories of customers, and that's ok too. The better you can understand your customers, the better you are able to self-market to them, and the better you are able to develop specific methods of keeping their attention, interest, and loyalty. This is known as "Customer Retention".

There are some things that must be considered in developing a customer retention plan. The level to which the customer feels involved with the company, the product, and the salesperson will affect his desire to stay with that company, product or salesperson. However, the customer must continue to be provided with attractive offers - When it comes to the attractiveness of offers presented to a customer, whether from you or from alternative sources, the customer is most likely to consider everything involved (such as the offer itself, the future benefits and the consequences of accepting the offer, the reputation of the company or product, etc.). Of course, price will also make quite a difference, even more so when the price difference is substantial.

## Customer Retention Programs

One way to keep your customers coming back is to develop customer retention programs. These are programs designed specifically to keep existing customers coming back whenever they choose to buy products that you sell. There are many types of customer retention programs, and you may only choose to use one type, or you may choose to use several.

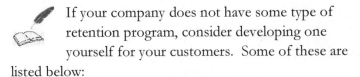

If your company does not have some type of retention program, consider developing one yourself for your customers. Some of these are listed below:

### Loyalty Programs

Loyalty programs are very common, and used by most major companies. These types of programs simply reward customers for shopping more frequently. Loyalty programs can be as simple as a punch-card on a coffee cup (as used by McDonalds Restaurants at the time of writing this book); but more commonly involve some form of point-system, where customers can gain points for every dollar value that they spend, and later redeem those points for something exciting.

## Customer Clubs

Customer Clubs are a great way to increase loyalty and customer satisfaction. These clubs are designed to give members special benefits that regular customers do not get. This also makes them feel "special".

## Customer Onboarding Programs

Customer Onboarding Programs are, in basic terms, orientation programs designed for new customers. These onboarding programs aim to provide some form of emotional satisfaction to customers during their first purchase, and usually extend to special privileges within the initial 60 to 90 days after first contact.

Consider giving a discount or special promotion to customers on their very first purchase with you (of course your keeping track of customers so that you can contact them again in the future right?). Consider also giving special deals to frequent purchasers, so that they keep coming back to you instead of going to the competition.

# Upselling & Cross-Selling

The primary aim of both upselling and cross-selling is to increase the amount that each customer spends, every time they make a purchase. Upselling involves either selling a better quality product than the one the customer originally wanted, or selling additional or add-on products and/or services that the customer may not have originally considered. Cross-selling is about selling the customer additional products, that may or may not be directly related to the product that he had originally intended to (or agreed to) buy.

There are methods in practice today when attempting to upsell or cross-sell a customer - Some of these include: Using assumption, or assuming the customer will want the upsell or cross-sell offer; using alternative-choice questioning; and bundling several products together (possibly for a price discount on the total package).

## Customer Life-Time Value

Customer life-time value is the total value of a customer over the life-time of his involvement with you; your company; or any particular product. There are essentially two main considerations involved when looking at customer life-time value: 1. Customer Life-Cycle; and 2. Product Life-Cycle

### Customer Life-Cycle

Customer life-cycle is the first and main consideration, and is simply defined as the duration in which the customer remains a customer. There are five basic phases of customer life-cycle... 1. Acquired Customer. 2. Moderate Customer. 3. Active Customer. 4. Repeat Customer. 5. Lapsed Customer.

This cycle also suggests that different strategies would be used to keep the customer. Sales skills are used to acquire a customer; while customer relations are used while the customer is moderate to active. Retention programs are used establish repeat customers; and finally effective management when the customer begins to seek alternative options as a lapsed customer.

**Product Life-Cycle**

The second consideration is the product life-cycle. Every product goes through stages from its inception into the market. Generally, these stages are represented as: 1. Introduction. 2. Growth. 3. Maturity. 4. Decline. Sometimes the product life-cycle is depicted with two extra phases: A Development phase prior to the introduction; and a Saturation phase after the maturity (before the decline).

The Perfect Sales Pro will understand which phase his customers are in, and use different tactics accordingly to keep customers interested in the product, product line or other potential offers. Work closely with the marketing and management team. For the sales professional, what is most important is the decline stage. When a product begins to decline, customers begin to seek other options. This is a crucial moment where the customer should be re-approached by the sales professional with a "new" suitable offer. If current customers are not approached prior to the end of a product life-cycle, those customers are likely to seek new products from an alternative source.

Every type of product has a certain life-cycle. For example, we know that people typically buy new homes every 20 years. They generally buy new cars every 5 years. We know that technology changes every 6 months, and people seek to update their computers every 1.5 years (on average). With knowledge about your product's life-cycle, you should aim to approach customers well before that life-cycle ends, so that when those customers are ready to make a purchase, they will have your new offer in forefront of their minds. Coupled with a pre-existing relationship, this could be very powerful.

Some customers, do not follow the general trend. Some customers prefer to have the newest models all the time, or the latest technology as soon as it becomes available. Some customers are just the opposite, they are skeptical about new things, and thus wait for products to be proven before they will buy. The Perfect Sales Pro will know his customer-base well, ensure frequent contact with them, and keep you on top of things when they decide to buy again.

## Partnerships and Affiliates

Another way to develop business growth in sales is to establish profitable partnerships and affiliates. Similar to having a strong social network, partnerships and affiliates provide you leverage, by having other people help you sell in exchange for a profit. The idea behind this, is that it is better to have 50% of ten sales, then 100% of one.

When a partnership exists, the partners will each have a direct stake in the outcome. These may be companies or salespeople in another industry, or perhaps a company in your distribution line, who stand to gain customers or profit when you do - This may involve an exchange of leads, an agreement for sales revenues, etc. Affiliates on the other hand, can cease to be an affiliate at any time. Affiliates are always paid directly by the salesperson, and this payment may be "per lead"; or it may be provided or "per prospect that is turned into a customer"; or it may be any other form of agreement.

Another method of growing your sales business is to sub-contract part of your sales process to someone else. You may want to sub-contract the prospecting or lead-generation phase, the qualifying phase, the presentation phase, or you may simply sub-contract the administrative and clerical duties. Sub-contracting allows you, as the salesperson, to focus more on what really counts... Closing more sales.

# Index

7 C 'S Of Effective Communication ....... 58
Active Voice .................. 65
Adductive Reasoning 163
Advantages ..................... 50
Advertising 55, 79, 81, 82, 83, 85, 92, 99, 100, 101, 119, 120
Advertising Location .... 85
Affiliates ....................... 189
Agitation ....................... 44
AIDA Formula .......... 120
Alternative Choice Close ..................................... 139
Alternative Choice Questions ................. 129
Ambiguity ...................... 61
Amiable .............. 26, 35, 36
Analytic .......................... 35
Analytical ....................... 26
Anger ..... 44, 45, 101, 110, 113, 179
Anger .............................. 44
Annoyance ..................... 44
Anticipation ................... 34
Aristotle .......................... 44
Associates And Affiliates ..................................... 31
Attending Problems .... 63
Attention ... 44, 45, 48, 55, 58, 59, 65, 67
Authority 32, 80, 153, 159
Bandwagon ................... 50

Bandwagon Effect ...... 156
Basic Business Skills ..... 18
Basic Needs ............ 28, 31
Behavioral Characteristics ..................................... 79
Being Better Needs 28, 31
Beliefs .. 62, 145, 149, 150, 164
Benefits 35, 50, 83, 97, 99, 113, 116, 117, 118, 120, 121, 122, 128, 158, 164, 166, 184, 186
Benefits .................... 44, 83
Bias ................................ 53
Body Language 58, 60, 67, 69, 71
Budget ........................... 80
Business Environment 34
Business Relationship Management ............... 31
Buyer's Remorse ........... 41
Buying Criteria ....... 47, 49
Buying Decision ... 37, 38, 42, 48, 51
Buying Factors . 44, 47, 51
Buying Factors .............. 44
Buying Factors .............. 44
Buying Process 37, 45, 51, 80
Buying Psychology ..... 158
Buying Reluctance ........ 49
Casual Listening ............ 62
Change ........................... 24

Chronological Flow ... 113
Close-Ended Questions ..................................... 126
Cold Call ....................... 79
Cold Lead .................... 181
Cold Market ................. 96
Cold-Call ..................... 121
Cold-Call Scripts .......... 96
Cold-Calling ...... 58, 81, 96
Cold-Calling Scripts ..... 96
Colors ............... 30, 84, 85
Comfort Zone .. 30, 51, 58
Commitment ..... 154, 155, 159, 166
Common-Ground ....... 59
Communicate ... 61, 68, 85
Communication .... 58, 60, 61, 62, 63, 64, 68, 82, 144, 151, 152, 158
Communication Skills 58, 62
Comparison Close ..... 140
Conditional Objection ..................................... 131
Confidence .................... 18
Confirmation Bias ........ 53
Consciously ...... 46, 60, 68, 71, 111, 132, 148
Consensus .. 102, 141, 157
Consensus .... 97, 156, 157
Consequences .......... 40, 43
Conservatism Bias ....... 53
Consistency .. 46, 155, 170
Consumer Psychology. 24
Contact Hypothesis ... 174
Contact Hypothesis ... 173

Cost / Benefit Ratio ..... 52
Cost Vs. Value .... 45, 137, 170
Criteria ..................... 49, 80
Cross-Selling ............... 186
Culture ........................... 33
Customer Buying Cycle ..................................... 38
Customer Clubs .......... 186
Customer Life-Cycle .. 187
Customer Life-Time Value ........................ 187
Customer Onboarding Programs ................... 186
Customer Participation ..................................... 184
Customer Retention ... 184
Customer Retention Programs ................... 185
Customer Service Skills ..................................... 176
David W. Merill ............ 26
Decision Making ........... 51
Deductive Reasoning . 163
Demographics ............... 78
Desire ...... 40, 44, 51, 100, 101, 102, 120, 121, 133, 150, 163, 174, 184
Desire .................. 102, 121
Desires ........................... 47
Differentiation ... 118, 140
Dilution Effect ... 174, 175
Dopamine ...................... 43
Drive .............................. 19
Driver ................ 26, 35, 36
Effective Questioning .. 36

Effort.............................. 45
Ego .................................. 47
Emotion.... 37, 38, 42, 43, 52, 54, 69, 149, 152, 162, 163, 164, 176, 179
Emotional ...................... 34
Emotional Control ...... 43
Emotional Involvement ..................................... 176
Emotional Reflection .. 62
Emotional Selling Proposition..... 118, 119
Emotional State ........... 43
Emotions ....................... 70
Empathy......................... 62
Energetic............35, 36, 95
Enthusiasm.................... 19
Estimated Purchase Date ...................................... 80
Exclusivity..........45, 46, 47
Expressive...................... 26
External Influence ....... 33
Extravert ....................... 37
Eye Gestures ........... 73, 74
Facial Expression.......... 70
Facial Signals ................ 67
False Stimulation........... 42
Familiar ......................... 46
Familiarity ............... 45, 46
Family And Friends..... 33
Fear 51, 58, 101, 102, 110, 156
Features ......................... 49
Feel-Good Chemicals . 43
Feel-Good Needs .. 28, 31
Flexible Personality ..... 60

Flow Structure ............113
Frame Of Mind.............70
Frustration....44, 101, 179
Funnel Questioning ..127, 135, 141
Games ...........................113
Gesture-Clusters.... 67, 69
Gestures......60, 63, 67, 69
Goal......................... 60, 61
Goals ... 19, 44, 45, 47, 49, 99, 102, 170, 174
Greed ............................102
Handshake.68, 71, 72, 73, 149
Handshake........ 69, 71, 72
Hate ..............................102
Head Gestures ...............67
Heightened Interest ...110
Heightened Interest Principle....................112
Hippocrates ............. 25, 26
Human Inertia...............50
Humors...........................25
Identification...... 144, 145
Immediacy .............. 45, 47
Impulse Buying.............42
Impulse Control ...........43
Impulse Decisions........43
Impulse Purchases........43
Inductive Reasoning ..163
Influence..33, 44, 87, 144, 149, 150, 152, 165, 181
Influence............. 144, 149
Influence Factors...........34
Influencers.....................33
Influences ..........25, 32, 51

Informational Objection ..................................... 131
Instant Gratification .... 37
Instant Reaction ........... 42
Interest .. 48, 80, 109, 110, 111, 112, 113, 115, 119, 121, 124, 125, 126, 137, 145, 146, 147, 184, 188
Internal Factors ............. 34
Internal Influence ........ 33
Internalization .............. 48
Internalization ............ 145
Interpersonal Styles 26, 35
Introvert ....................... 37
Irritation ........................ 44
Jack The Ripper ........... 26
Joe Girard ................... 175
Lead-Generation .......... 77
Leading Questions ...... 37, 127
Legal Issues .................... 33
Limbic System ............... 43
Link ................................. 86
Link-Building ................. 86
Listening ........................ 62
Listening Skills ............. 58
Location ................... 33, 49
Logic .... 37, 38, 43, 52, 54, 119, 151, 152, 162, 164, 179
Logic ..................... 162, 163
Love ..................... 102, 169
Love And Belonging ... 28
Loyalty Programs ....... 185
Mark Mccormack ......... 19
Mary Kelly .................... 26
Maslow's Hierarchy 28, 30
Matching ......... 50, 95, 148
Mcdonald's ............. 32, 33
Micro-Expressions ...... 70, 149
Micro-Gestures ............. 67
Similar Situation Close ..................................... 141
Minor Objections ....... 133
Mirroring ...................... 148
Mood ...................... 65, 66
Mood Alteration .... 65, 66
Moscow ......................... 21
Motivation . 19, 27, 28, 32, 33, 102, 158
Motivators ..................... 32
Narrative Mode ............. 64
Narrative Modes ........... 66
Narrative Voice ............. 64
Needs ............................ 45
Neural Map ................... 22
Non-Specific Communication ........ 61
Non-Verbal Communication . 58, 67
Objection ..... 77, 124, 129, 130, 131, 132, 133, 134, 135, 136
Objection Chunking ... 135
Objection Handling .. 133, 134, 158
Open Gesture ............... 69
Open Minded ................ 69
Open-Ended Questions ..................................... 126

Optional Buying Factors ...... 49
Or Lead-Generation.. 190
Organization .................. 20
Pain ..... 44, 47, 53, 84, 102
Partnerships ........... 31, 189
Parts Of A Speech ....... 63
Passion ................... 84, 101
Passive Voice ................. 65
Peers ............................... 44
Perceived Value ............ 45
Persistence ..................... 19
Personal Preferences ... 35, 51
Personalities .................. 35
Personality 19, 25, 26, 27, 35, 94, 95, 124, 145, 149, 152
Personality Differences 35
Personality Preference 36
Personality Preference Factors ........................ 35
Personality Profiling .... 25, 26
Personality Style .......... 164
Personality Traits ......... 25
Personality Type ... 35, 36, 51, 158
Perspective ..................... 49
Persuade ....... 81, 144, 151, 152, 158, 160, 163
Persuasion ...... 19, 60, 144, 151, 152, 158, 162, 165, 166
Persuasion Statement .. 97

Physiological Needs .... 28, 29
Pleasure ................... 47, 53
Point Of View ............... 54
Politics ............................ 33
Post-Purchase Syndrome ....................................... 41
Preference Factors ....... 36
Preferences ............. 35, 37
Prefrontal Cortex .......... 43
Preliminary Buying Factors ................ 44, 48
Presentation ...... 48, 55, 63
Price ............................... 49
Primacy - Recency Effect ..................................... 109
Primary Buying Factors .............................. 45, 48
Prioritize ........................ 21
Prioritizing .................... 52
Procedures .................... 20
Procrastination .............. 21
Product Life-Cycle ..... 188
Product Life-Cycle .... 187, 188
Pros And Cons ............. 52
Prospect ..... 18, 22, 34, 36, 37, 40, 44, 46, 47, 48, 49, 50, 51, 52, 54, 55, 59, 63, 67, 74, 76, 77, 78, 79, 80, 81, 82, 83, 92, 93, 94, 96, 97, 98, 99, 100, 112, 114, 116, 117, 118, 119, 124, 126, 127, 128, 129, 130, 131, 132, 133, 134, 135, 136,

137, 138, 139, 140, 141, 144, 145, 146, 148, 149, 150, 151, 152, 154, 156, 157, 158, 159, 163, 164, 175, 178, 181, 189
Prospecting ...... 77, 79, 92, 190
Proxemic Communication . 67, 68
Proxemics ...................... 68
Psychographics ............. 78
Psychological ................ 34
Punctuation ................... 66
Purchase Criteria .......... 49
Quality ............................ 49
Questions ................ 48, 54
Questions ...................... 36
Rapport 27, 59, 60, 67, 73, 94, 144, 145, 146, 147, 148, 151, 169, 171, 178
Rapport ........ 59, 144, 169
RAS ...................... 111, 112
Reactive Buying ............. 43
Reactive Buying Process .................................. 42, 43
Reactive Process .......... 38
Reasoning ... 151, 162, 163
Reciprocity 147, 150, 156, 170
Recurring Desire .......... 44
Referrals ........................ 77
Referrals ........................ 77
Rejection ....................... 58
Relationship ..... 19, 26, 27, 31, 62, 92, 124, 126, 127, 145, 147, 150, 154, 156, 158, 163, 166, 169, 170, 171, 172, 173, 174, 176, 177, 184, 189
Relationship ................. 170
Relationship Development. ........... 19
Relationships ................. 19
Relevancy ...................... 48
Relevancy ...................... 47
Relevant ........................ 48
Reluctant ....................... 25
Reticular Activating System ...................... 111
Reticular Activator .... 111, 112
Robert Cialdini ............. 152
Roger H. Reid ............... 26
Safe ................................ 30
Safety And Security ...... 28
Safety Need ............ 29, 31
Sales ..... 19, 20, 22, 24, 34, 38, 40, 51, 61, 76, 77, 79, 85, 92, 93, 127, 137, 144, 162, 165, 189, 190
Sales ............................ 1, 80
Sales Cycle .............. 76, 77
Sales Funnel ................... 77
Sales Letter .... 81, 82, 100, 101, 102, 103
Sales Letter ... 48, 100, 120
Sales Literature ..... 92, 100
Sales Plan ....................... 20
Sales Presentation ...... 116, 120
Sales Presentation ....... 116
Sales Presentations ..... 116

Sales Process ..... 36, 37, 92
Scarcity ............ 55, 57, 158
Secondary Buying Factors ........................ 49
Security Needs ............. 28
Selective Perception .... 54, 55
Self-Actualization ......... 28
Self-Actualization Needs ...................................... 31
Self-Concept .................. 19
Self-Development 18, 158
Self-Esteem ............. 19, 28
Self-Esteem Needs ...... 30
Self-Improvement ....... 18
Sensory Activity ........... 42
Sensory Gating ............. 62
Sex Appeal ..................... 84
Sharp Angle Close ..... 140
Similar ............................. 19
Situation ........................ 50
Situational Change ....... 33
Situational Influence .... 33
Situational Objection 130
Small Talk ................ 58, 59
Social Needs ........... 28, 31
Social Networking ..... 181
Social Niche .................. 30
Social Status .................. 33
Special ................ 46, 47, 55
Specific ........................... 48
Specificity ...................... 60
Stage Fright ......... 107, 122
Standard Buying Process .............................. 38, 43
Statement Of Benefits. 83
Stepping Stone .............. 20
Story Plot ...................... 114
Story Type .................... 115
Sub-Contracting .......... 190
Sub-Groups .................... 25
Sub-Routines ................. 22
Supply And Demand ... 33
Syllogistic Reasoning .. 163
Systematize .................... 20
Systematized ................. 22
Systems .................... 20, 21
Tag Questions ............. 127
Target Market ... 32, 48, 87
Target Marketing .. 78, 85, 86, 101
Telephone Sales ..... 92, 94
The Ben Franklin Effect ................................... 172
The Dead Fish .............. 72
The Dominator ............. 72
The Glove ...................... 72
The Master Sales Manual . 11, 14, 15, 26, 62, 115, 124, 127, 144
The Self-Interest Principle ................... 147
Themes .................... 83, 85
Thomas Bond ................ 26
Time ..... 33, 45, 46, 47, 52
Time Of Impulse .......... 42
Transition ...................... 66
Transitional Phrase ....... 67
Trigger Events .............. 44
Trust .... 19, 29, 49, 59, 60, 64, 72, 93, 94, 137, 145, 148, 150, 151, 154

Unconsciously ..... 60, 112, 132, 148
Unique Selling Proposition ............. 118
Upselling ...................... 186
Value .. 40, 45, 46, 83, 112, 136, 137, 138, 140, 156, 157, 166, 170, 171, 173
Values ... 78, 149, 150, 164
Vocal Style ...... 94, 95, 148
Warm Lead .................. 181
Warm Market ................ 96
Word Of Mouth ........... 33
Writing ........................... 63
Written Communication ...................................... 64
Yes-Set Close .............. 141
Zig Ziglar ................ 20, 49

Proof

Made in the USA
Charleston, SC
25 October 2014